the low-fat, low-carb
SOUTHWEST
COOKBOOK

the low-fat, low-carb SOUTHWEST COOKBOOK

New Edition

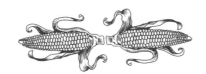

anne lindsay greer mccann

TAYLOR TRADE PUBLISHING

Lanham New York Dallas Boulder Toronto Oxford

Published by Taylor Trade Publishing
An imprint of The Rowman & Littlefield Publishing Group, Inc.
4501 Forbes Boulevard, Suite 200
Lanham, Maryland 20706

Interior design by Piper E. Furbush

Distributed by National Book Network

Library of Congress Cataloging-in-Publication Data
McCann, Anne.
   The low-fat, low-carb Southwest cookbook / Anne Lindsay Greer McCann.— New ed.
      p. cm.
   Includes index.
   ISBN 1-58979-178-9 (pbk. : alk. paper)
   1. Low-fat diet—Recipes. 2. Low-carbohydrate diet—Recipes. 3. Cookery, American—Southwestern style. I. McCann, Greer. II. Title.
   RM237.7.L565 2004
   641.5'6384—dc22   2004021047

⊗™   The paper used in this publication meets the minimum requirements of
American National Standard for Information Sciences—Permanence of
Paper for Printed Library Materials, ANSI/NISO Z39.48–1992.
Manufactured in the United States of America.

To Don and Will, with love and admiration

And especially to Kelly

CONTENTS

Foreword

Stephan Pyles

Anne Lindsay Greer McCann is a true visionary and was the first person to expose the country to Southwestern Cuisine. She was also the catalyst for bringing together its key practitioners who went on to found one of the most significant regional styles of cooking in American culinary history. I still can remember with great clarity the dinners she hosted at her home twenty years ago for me, Dean Fearing, Amy Ferguson, Avner Samuel, and Robert Del Grande. We were all experimenting wildly back then, and she seemed to bring focus to a food movement that had very little structure or form. It was at one of these dinners that we cooperatively developed the menu for the 1984 inaugural dinner for the Texas Hill Country Wine and Food Festival, which has become one of the most successful and respected culinary celebrations in America today.

Anne's dedication and vast knowledge of the subject through years of research and recipe development is evident through her prolific writings. After more than two decades, her style remains distinct and unique among the many stars of the movement. She has inspired an entire generation of American chefs who have become famous for cooking with the flavors of the Southwest. Bobby Flay once told me that Anne's book *Foods of the Sun*, was an impetus in the early development of his now celebrated cooking style.

Anne's latest undertaking is right on target with today's interest (and sometimes obsession) in more healthful food preparation. She has blended two major trends—low-fat, low-carb and big, bold flavors. She rightfully demonstrates that Southwestern Cuisine is inherently quite healthful and wholesome, deriving its flavors from chiles, salsas, and grilled or smoked foods. By eliminating most rice and potato dishes she successfully ties into the single most significant dietary change in America today, the restriction of carbohydrate intake. In this book, she proves that a healthful, non-fattening diet does not have to be mutually exclusive from one that is robust and flavorful.

Without Anne's vision and exposure to the foods of this region in the early 1980s, there simply wouldn't be the distinct and comprehensive understanding and appreciation of the cuisine that exists today. She is truly the unsung hero of the Southwestern Cuisine movement in America. This book just further establishes that hero status.

HIGH IN FLAVOR—LOW IN FAT

Whether you call it Contemporary Mexican or Southwest, the spirited flavors of tortilla specialties and grilled foods create an insatiable desire for salsas, quesadillas, and smoked or grilled
foods. Surprisingly, the main ingredients in these foods (corn, rice, beans, chiles, tomatoes, and
tortillas) are low in fat and high in nutritional value.

However, some are high in carbohydrates. Many popular diets severely limit carbohydrates,
including most fruits and vegetables. The recipes in this book do not eliminate carbohydrates,
but keep them within a reasonable fat, calorie, and carbohydrate count. While not supported by
scientific evidence or extensive research, I do believe that limiting fats, carbohydrates, and calories will allow you to enjoy most of the foods of the Southwest. Many fast-food restaurants have
discovered that a flour tortilla is low in fat and carbs and tout them for low-carb wraps. Cheese,
a main ingredient in traditional Mexican cooking, is more of an accent in most of the recipes in
this book. Those recipes that rely on cheese (Queso and some of the dips) have been reduced
in calories by using low-fat cheeses or less cheese.

Most important, the seasonings, chiles, varied salsas, and vinaigrettes, give satisfying flavor
to the foods. This is a different way of cooking with some new ingredients. You will learn many
ways to use chiles, salsas, and even cheese to give personality to your dishes. You will find a
shortage of rice recipes and no recipes with pasta or white potatoes. I find personally that if I
omit these foods, including white bread, muffins, and pies, an occasional indulgence in chocolate or other light dessert makes little difference in my dress size. Desserts fall into a "save and
spend" philosophy . . . save to spend on desserts.

COOKING LIGHT

Lighter, low-fat cooking can be achieved in several ways. Use lean cuts of meat and remove all
visible fat from meats, fish, and poultry. Use oil sparingly, or purchase a small spray device from
a cookware shop. Oil or butter has about 120 calories per tablespoon and 12 fat grams. Dramatic amounts of fat are saved by using a variety of cooking sprays.

Cooking sprays have many uses other than sautéing. Butter-flavored sprays are good for
softening or baking tortillas. The olive-oil sprays may be used on tossed salad greens, grilled
vegetables, fish, and poultry. Many of the recipes for tacos, enchiladas, fajitas, and grilled fish
emphasize seasoning, herbs, and chiles in place of fats and oils. Fresh fruits and vegetables
are used generously in main dishes and accompaniments to add flavor instead of fat. Cutting
creamy salad dressings with water also saves calories and makes little difference in the taste.
Most purchased, refrigerated dressings are too thick anyway. Using low- or reduced-fat
cheeses saves calories as does using less cheese. Many salads may not need any dressing
at all, or much less than we are used to.

Salsas, vinaigrettes, and rich-tasting meat sauces replace high-fat butter or cream sauces. The Pico de Gallo vinaigrette (p. 28) and the Whiskey Sauce (p. 136) can be used on many different dishes, adding flavor without fat.

CALORIES, CARBS, AND FAT

All recipes have been analyzed for fat, carbs, and calories. There is always some variation, even among professional analysts, depending on the products that are used. In this book, all counts are rounded out to the nearest decimal and are to be viewed as approximate. This is not a "diet" book for restrictive diets. Rather, it is a book of healthful recipes that reduces calories, carbs, and fats. I don't think cooking or eating is much fun if you have to weigh or calculate everything you eat. Better to have an awareness of where the high-fat, carb, and calorie counts are and work around them. Here are some tips:

➡ Anything served in a taco can be served in a lettuce cup . . . if entertaining, you can offer a choice. Your guests will thank you!

➡ Cheese dips can be served with vegetable scoops as well as low-fat crackers or toasted tortillas.

➡ If using a butter sauce, use a very small amount, or whisk in some diced chiles, tomatoes, sun-dried tomatoes, herbs, or a little chicken broth . . . you will need less butter.

Always read labels when shopping. There is a significant difference in carb, calorie, and fat counts for the same item. Flour tortillas are one example. Some "light" items have more carbs or fat than their original version. Many energy bars have as many calories as a candy bar. Opt for freshness as much as possible—canned or packaged foods can be loaded with carbs and fat.

EATING LIGHT WHILE EATING OUT

Eating light when eating out is another challenge. Armed with some fat information and low-fat cooking techniques, it's easier to see where the fat is in Southwest food. While table salsa is "free," the chips are loaded with fat and calories, and it is easy to consume hundreds of calories before you order your dinner. I'm not suggesting you give up your weekly Southwest or Mexican meal, but here are a few suggestions for lightening up:

➡ Order soft corn tortillas instead of (or in addition to) the fried ones.

➡ Start with tortilla soup, gazpacho, or any non-cream soup . . . it will curb the hunger.

➡ Tell the waiter you don't want your fajitas "sizzled" (that's done with added fat).

➡ Omit bread, pasta, and white potatoes, and limit desserts.

➡ Use salsa on a taco salad, order *all* dressings on the side (you can dilute them with water), and try some salads without dressing (for example, Cobb Salad, Greek Salad).

➡ Beware of anything sautéed . . . restaurants *don't* use vegetable coating sprays. Ask if fish is grilled on an open grill or a flat top grill. Big difference.

➡ Order vegetables steamed. Grilled vegetables in a restaurant, especially eggplant and Portobello mushrooms, can be soaked in fat.

➡ Southwest restaurants are second only in popularity to Italian. Even hard-core Tex-Mex eateries have lightened up and offer more choices, including grilled chicken, seafood items, and entree salads. The fun, irresistible flavors and festive personality of Southwest food can fit into a fat-conscious lifestyle.

DO AHEAD OR QUICK RECIPES

Many excellent cooks find themselves too busy with motherhood or work, or both, or well-deserved recreation, to spend a lot of time shopping and cooking. The good news is that supermarkets offer many excellent prepared items, partially prepared items, and specialty foods that previously had to be cooked from scratch. Most of the recipes have been revised for easier preparation and many use purchased ingredients.

Advance preparation instructions are given when appropriate. Suggestions for a well-stocked pantry and refrigerator/freezer are given to aid in everyday cooking as well as entertaining. Here are a few suggestions:

➡ Keep roasted chiles and bell peppers in resealable bags in the freezer. All you have to do is thaw and peel them.

➡ Pour Raspberry Chipotle Sauce (p. 133) over light or low-fat cream cheese for an easy appetizer.

➡ Add a little grated smoked Gouda cheese and diced jalapeño chiles to purchased pimiento cheese and use the mixture to fill celery sticks.

➡ Whip two egg whites (stiff) and add to 1 cup pimiento cheese, mound on toast rounds, and bake at 475° for 5 minutes for a quick hot appetizer.

➡ For a quick marinade, combine one 12-oz. bottle of Italian dressing with ⅛ cup soy sauce and the juice of one lime or lemon. This adds both flavor and moisture to boneless chicken breasts.

➡ Buy chicken salad, add a few toasted, chopped pecans, and mound in phyllo cups for a quick appetizer. Drizzle with a little Green Goddess salad dressing or a dollop of Raspberry Chipotle Sauce. These can also be heated in a 375° oven for 8 to 10 minutes; drizzle with sauce just before serving.

➡   Buy frozen chicken on skewers and serve them with one or two salsas or Chile Poblano Cream (p. 40) and a salsa in place of the Asian sauce they are packaged with.

➡   Drain ½ cup of sun-dried tomatoes packed in oil and press between paper towels to absorb most of the oil. Mix with ½ cup toasted sliced almonds and ¼ cup chopped chives or green scallions. Serve with room temperature goat cheese or low-fat cream cheese and low-carb crackers.

➡   Fill endive leaves with a slice of fresh pear and top with crumbled mild blue cheese and a few candied chopped walnuts.

➡   Wrap blanched asparagus tips in thinly sliced peppered smoked turkey and serve with a jalapeño mustard dip.

➡   Combine equal amounts of sun-dried tomatoes with Pico de Gallo (p. 28) and put it in toasted, mini phyllo shells. Top with a dollop of light cream cheese and goat cheese, mixed together in equal amounts. Heat in 375° oven for 5–6 minutes.

➡   Wrap miniature low-fat sausages in phyllo dough and bake 10 minutes at 375°, or until hot. Serve with a spicy mustard or BBQ sauce.

➡   Buy frozen chicken taquitos, spray them with olive-oil spray, and heat according to package directions. Serve with guacamole and a salsa from your favorite Mexican restaurant, or Chipotle Ranch Dressing (p. 25).

Fortunately, you can buy many excellent salsas, guacamole, roasted chickens, and pre-packaged greens, making all food preparation easier.

1
The Basics

Woe to the cook whose sauce has no sting.

—Chaucer

Certain cooking techniques and recipes can dramatically reduce fats and oils while adding delicious flavors to foods. Try the tips and recipes that follow for preparing tortillas, chilies, soup stocks, and beans. Soon they will become basic procedures you will use again and again in countless recipes.

Food presentation and garnish is equally important, and the fun, whimsical nature of Southwest food, coupled with colorful natural ingredients, lends itself to creative garnishes that can almost always be low in fat.

Seasoning is very important in all cooking—it's what gives food "soul" and makes it memorable and satisfying. A pinch of cayenne gives cornmeal crepes personality. Cilantro and green chile pestos will brighten all your sauces and fillings. Smoky, spicy stocks liven up soups, chili, and enchilada sauces.

CHILES: FACT, FOLKLORE, AND FUN

Chiles are named for their color (chile colorado), their use (chile de ristra), their shape (chile ancho), their place of origin (chile Anaheim or Chimaya), or their hotness (numero 6). No other ingredient resists standardization with such persistence or has enjoyed almost ritualistic attention. Although originally used to enhance an otherwise bland diet, chiles quickly became one of the first health foods and were used for medicinal purposes. They were once also used as currency, and as an aid to discourage thumb sucking in children. Chiles were thought to cure everything from a common cold to indifference towards romance. Current research suggests there could be more truth than folklore in such beliefs. Chiles may block cancer-causing compounds found in meats and may increase your metabolism, hastening weight loss. Some statements about chiles remain undisputed:

- ➡ Chiles have no fat and are high in vitamins A and C (higher than citrus).
- ➡ Chiles are low in calories.
- ➡ Chiles serve as a natural meat preservative by retarding the oxidation of fats.
- ➡ Chiles add personality and flavor to a variety of foods.
- ➡ Green chiles are more nutritious than red chiles.

- Chiles contain bioflavonoids, thought to be cancer fighting.
- Once you include chiles in your cooking, you might possibly become addicted.

This book limits chiles to a few varieties, all easily found in your supermarket. Many chili powders, dried chiles, and fresh chiles are also available in specialty markets. Don't let the spelling confuse you—in general the chile is a pepper and chili is a stew, even though chili powder is spelled "chili." Most commercial brands, particularly generic chili powder and cayenne pepper, will be blends of various chiles. When cooking with chile pods, you will find it necessary to balance the earthy, sometimes bitter flavors with brown sugar, dried or fresh fruits, maple syrup, citrus, or vinegar. Tomatoes or tomatillos are often used to balance chili sauces and reduce the heat. Fats, such as bacon fat, cream, or butter, are a natural balance for chiles. That's why cheese, chili sauces, and copious amounts of sour cream are such tasty combinations. I've avoided these techniques in the recipes or limited their use to lower the fat and calories without sacrificing the delicious flavors that make these foods irresistible. I was surprised and delighted to find that a little cheese goes a long way, and many of the new low-fat or fat-free products are quite acceptable.

Dried Chiles

Chile Ancho: This is the dried poblano chile that has a distinctive wrinkled skin and flat wide shape. It is the chile used for chili con carne. It can be mild to hot with an earthy flavor. Toast chiles before using in a 300° oven for about 8 minutes, then soak in water to rehydrate. Remove stems, seeds, and skin before using in soups, stews, or sauces.

Red Chile: The dried Anaheim or New Mexico chile has a smooth skin and long narrow shape. Rumored to be as unpredictable as a woman, it varies from very mild to incendiary, with an addictive flavor. Prepare in the same way described above.

Chipotle: This chile is usually found canned, although its recent popularity has encouraged grocers to stock it in a dried state. Canned chipotles are packed in adobo, a smoky, very hot sauce. This is the dried jalapeño, which gives you a clue to its heat level. Use it sparingly and you'll love the flavors. This chile is a favorite among chefs for barbecue and meat sauces. I prefer to use the adobo sauce in most recipes.

Fresh Chiles

Fresh chiles should be roasted and peeled to remove bitter, tough skins. Protect your hands with gloves or a generous coating of oil. Capsaicin, the substance that makes chiles hot, resists soap and water and remains on your hands a long time, so don't rub your eyes after cutting or peeling chiles. If blending or disposing of seeds in a disposal, try not to inhale deeply or you might lose your voice temporarily. You can see where the saying "It took a brave man to eat the first jalapeño, but a Texan to eat the second" might have come from. Don't let these cautionary instructions prevent you from working with fresh chiles. Your reward will be spirited flavors that give personality and soul to your cooking.

Green Chile: This is a smooth-skinned, light green chile shaped like a small banana. Both its name and heat level are not easily recognized, but in general New Mexico chiles are significantly hotter than Anaheim chiles. This is the chile used for canning. The skin is thinner than the poblano chile, making these chiles more difficult to work with when peeling or stuffing. They can be mild to hot.

Poblano Chile: This is a large, dark green chile shaped somewhat like a bell. Its thick skin and rich flavor make it ideal for stuffing or dicing and for adding flavor to soups, sauces, and quesadillas. Heat levels will vary with the season and growing area, but the poblano chile is usually moderately hot with a pleasant heat level. When dried, this becomes the chile ancho.

Jalapeño: This chile is small and dark green or red. It has a thick flesh and is hot to very hot. Jalapeños are often canned or sliced and pickled in glass jars. The heat is in the seeds and veins, so removing these allows you to enjoy the flavor with less bite. Jalapeños have a forward, lip-searing heat that can be tempered with milk, sour cream, or something sweet. Water is useless. There is a new, bright red jalapeño-shaped chile that is mild and makes a wonderful garnish.

Serrano: This is a very thin, light green chile that is as hot as the jalapeño. Although the heat is less "forward," it builds with each bite. It does not need to be roasted and peeled when used in relishes and salsas. However, you will want to remove the skin if it has been roasted. These chiles are hot to very hot.

Habanero: These are small bell-shaped chiles in bright green, red, and orange colors and are extremely hot. They may be used to make colorful accent creams and sauces (see the garnish section) or "conversational" table decorations.

To Roast and Peel Fresh Green Chiles

You may use your broiling element, electric range, gas burner, or outdoor grill.

Broiling: Preheat the broiler on the highest temperature. First cut the chiles in half and discard seeds and stems. Place the chiles on a flat cookie sheet, directly under the broiler, and leave the door ajar. Roast until lightly charred and then turn to char all surfaces. Bell peppers can be roasted in the same way.

Range Top: Place a heat-proof rack atop your element and turn the heat to high. Place the chiles on the rack and roast until lightly charred. Turn the chiles to char all sides. They may jump a bit or sizzle and crackle—this is normal.

Gas Range: Spear chiles with a fork and place over the flame, turning to roast, and char all sides.

Outdoor Grill: Roasting chiles over an outdoor charcoal grill will give the best flavor and aroma. Place them on the grill, close to the coals, and roast until lightly charred. Turn to char all sides. An indoor grill also works well; however, the charcoal flavors are absent.

In all cases, place the hot, charred chiles in a freezer bag and seal tightly. Let the chiles "steam" for 5 to 10 minutes, then remove stems and seeds, and peel. Chiles may be frozen, unpeeled, in freezer bags for a later use; however, the texture will not be as firm.

Roasting chiles indoors is a project that can set off your smoke alarm, so be forewarned but not dissuaded. The aromatic flavors of fresh roasted chiles are well worth the effort.

MEXICAN CHEESES

Many Mexican cheeses are now available at most supermarkets. Their flavor and melting texture are very different from other cheeses. The following cheeses are used in the book. Fat grams, calories, and carbohydrates are for one ounce of cheese. Most traditional recipes use considerably more cheese than is really necessary. I have used enough for the required flavor and texture, keeping both fat and calories reduced.

- ➡ Cotija: A crumbly cheese suitable for salads, to top chalupas or enchiladas
  Fat Grams 8   Calories 100   Carbohydrates 0
- ➡ Manchego: A flavorful soft cheese with buttery taste and good melting qualities
  Fat Grams 0   Calories 90   Carbohydrates 8
- ➡ Queso Fresca: A crumbly cheese similar in taste to Feta, only less acidic and not as salty
  Fat Grams 6   Calories 80   Carbohydrates 0
- ➡ Anejo: An aged cheese, similar to Parmesan, made with skim milk
  Fat Grams 1   Calories 100   Carbohydrates 1
- ➡ Oaxaca: Melts quickly with rich buttery taste
  Fat Grams 6   Calories 80   Carbohydrates 0

GARNISHES AND ACCENT SALSAS

Restaurateurs and chefs spend as much time and energy in the presentation of their dishes as in their preparation. Contemporary Southwest dishes invite colorful and sometimes spicy garnishes. Chefs discovered the squirt bottle, and zig-zag adornments evolved in a variety of colors and flavors. Roasted chiles can be blended into colorful creams to garnish soups, salads, or tortilla specialties. See the recipes for Cilantro Cream on page 22, Chile Poblano Cream, page 40, or Chipotle Ranch Dressing, page 25. The availability of red and blue tortillas, a variety of lettuces, bell peppers, chiles, and tomatoes in brilliant shades of red, orange, and yellow, all contribute to the visual appeal of Southwest food. I suspect the popularity of black beans is in part due to the color contrast they provide on the plate.

A sprinkling of crumbled feta cheese, thinly sliced radishes, or a colorful salsa can transform an enchilada plate. Rice flecked with a variety of vegetables or chile-studded spoon bread served on a fringed tamale husk creates a plate with visual appeal. Spicy creams made from chiles or chili powder can be drizzled over mild sauces or soups. Tomatillo husks or bell peppers may be used as "ramekins" for salsas or side dishes. Dried or green corn husks can line a pie plate for a tamale pie or contain a sweet or savory corn pudding.

Most of the edible garnishes that follow have little or no fat and supply color, texture, and contrasting flavors to the Southwest dishes in this book. Make use of the wonderful array of chiles and natural ingredients to give your food a professional, appetizing appearance.

Crispy Greens

Thinly sliced lettuces of contrasting colors—red tip leaf lettuce, romaine, red cabbage, radicchio, spinach, or green leaf lettuce—may be topped with a sprinkling of toasted tortilla strips or pumpkin seeds and diced tomatoes. Use to garnish enchilada plates, combination plates, or entrées.

Spicy Creams

Roasted chiles or chili powders can be blended into colorful creams to garnish soups, salads, or tortilla specialties. They are quite hot, so use them on milder soups or sauces or to serve as a dipping sauce for quesadillas or tortilla chips. Purée the roasted, seeded chiles in a blender with 1 to 2 ounces light or low-fat cream cheese and use a little chicken broth to aid blending. Blend until very smooth, adding 1 to 2 tablespoons warm safflower oil as the blender runs. Season with salt, pepper, and a squeeze of lime juice. For green chiles, add generous sprigs of parsley to intensify the color. For red chiles, add a small amount of tomato paste.

If using cayenne pepper or chili powder, heat 1 to 2 tablespoons oil in a small skillet and add 2 tablespoons powder. Stir a few seconds, then transfer to a blender jar and blend with 1 tablespoon tomato paste, 1 ounce light or low-fat cream cheese and 2 to 3 tablespoons chicken broth. Use enough broth to make a consistency of heavy cream. Season to taste with salt and pepper. Dried chile pods may also be used to make accent creams. Simmer them in hot water until softened. Seed, stem, and peel the chiles. Purée in a blender with enough chicken broth to make a smooth, thick sauce. Strain to remove skin. Add 1 to 2 tablespoons maple syrup to balance flavors. Season with salt and pepper.

Salsas

All of the fresh salsas make tasty and colorful garnishes for many dishes. Choose complementary colors and flavors. A simple combination of diced jicama, fresh corn, cilantro, and fresh lime juice is delicious with red or chili enchilada sauces. A simple Jicama Salsa (p. 39), enhances a quesadilla plate.

A Papaya Salsa, page 36, complements grilled or broiled fish with fewer calories, fats, or carbs than a rich butter sauce. Try a black bean salsa in place of beans. Use your imagination!

Edible Garnishes

Californians are fond of sour cream and black olives to garnish many Cal-Mex dishes. Crema (p. 21) makes a good substitute and a neutral background for olives, green scallions, toasted tortilla strips, or thin strips of spinach or lettuces. There are a variety of low-fat cheeses on the market you can substitute for the traditional longhorn cheddar or Monterey jack cheese. The slightly tart, salty flavor of low-fat feta or goat cheese is delicious with many dishes, particularly those using tomatillos, wild mushrooms, chili sauces, or seafood. The new, light processed American cheese makes it possible to make a significantly lighter Chile con Queso (p. 41). Think of cheese as a garnish—you'll save fat and calories.

Corn Husks

Dried and green corn husks may be used to make "containers" for side dishes or to line a pie pan for tamale pie. Both need to first be soaked in hot water to soften them. Many enchilada casseroles are enhanced by attractive "fringed" corn husks around the edges.

To make individual corn husk containers, use a large husk. Clean and soak the husk until it is pliable. Tie a string or thin strip of husk around the narrow end, leaving about 3 inches above the tie. Fringe the ends and place in a flame to brown the edges. (They will not burn easily because they are wet.) Turn the wide portion inside out. (This helps maintain the shape.) To hold their shape, freeze the husk containers until ready to use. Use the husks for salads, spoon bread, or cornmeal pudding.

Toasted Nuts

Toasted nuts can be part of a dish or a garnish. This technique vastly improves the taste of all nuts. Preheat oven to 325°.

Coat a cookie sheet with an olive-oil cooking spray. Arrange nuts (almonds, pine nuts, pecans, walnuts) in a single layer. Lightly spray again and season with freshly ground sea salt. When you chop the toasted nuts, it is useful to place them in a strainer and shake the strainer to remove the "dust." The result is crisp, chopped nuts.

Bake 10 to 12 minutes, or until slightly crisp and very lightly browned. Watch carefully as they can burn quickly.

Staples

The following items are useful to have on hand in your pantry, refrigerator, or freezer. Some involve a little advance preparation but will make cooking recipes with chiles much easier. Others are useful to make quick sauces, seasonings, or appetizers.

Pantry

➡ Olive-oil, vegetable-oil, and butter-flavored cooking sprays (or buy a spray bottle made for this purpose)

➡ Light olive oil
➡ Extra virgin olive oil
➡ Safflower oil
➡ Chili oil
➡ Rice wine vinegar
➡ Balsamic vinegar
➡ Sherry vinegar
➡ Italian dressing mix
➡ Ranch dressing mix

➡ Au jus gravy mix (Knorr Swiss)
➡ Taco seasoning
➡ Chili powder (Gebhardt's)
➡ BBQ seasoning
➡ Steak seasoning (Montreal)
➡ Chicken seasoning (Montreal)
➡ Chicken bouillon powder

➡ Bird's Custard Powder

➡ Assorted picante sauces (many flavors are available)
➡ Raspberry chipotle sauce
➡ Canned shrimp
➡ Black beans (ranch style)
➡ Pinto beans
➡ Chicken broth
➡ Beef broth
➡ Green chiles (canned, diced)
➡ Chipotle chiles (canned)
➡ Tomatoes and green chiles (Ro*tel)
➡ Diced tomatoes (not stewed)
➡ Artichoke hearts
➡ Sun-dried tomatoes (dry or packed in oil)

➡ Margarita mix
➡ Tequila

- ➡ Triple Sec
- ➡ Kahlua

- ➡ Almonds (sliced)
- ➡ Pecans (whole)

- ➡ Taco shells (regular and mini)
- ➡ Cornmeal (white and yellow)
- ➡ Grits (not instant)

Freezer
- ➡ Light non-dairy, whipped topping
- ➡ Phyllo cups (mini)
- ➡ Phyllo Dough (sheets)
- ➡ Roasted poblano chiles
- ➡ Roasted red and yellow bell peppers
- ➡ Cilantro pesto
- ➡ Basil pesto

Refrigerator
- ➡ Cream cheese (light or low-fat)
- ➡ Assorted low-fat or light cheeses
- ➡ Light butter (Land O' Lakes)
- ➡ Non-fat sour cream (Land O' Lakes)
- ➡ Ranch dressing (T. Margarita's)
- ➡ Caesar dressing (T. Margarita's)

- ➡ Garlic
- ➡ Shallots
- ➡ Onions

OVEN-FRIED TORTILLAS

Chalupas, chips and salsa, taco shells, and chiliquilas—they are all fried, resulting in fat and calories. The good news is that one corn tortilla is only about 50 calories with 1 gram of fat. The bad news is one small chip is about 30 calories with 1 to 2 grams of fat. One way to cut down on fat calories is to oven toast your own tortillas. The following instructions will tell you how to prepare basic chips and strips as well as decorative bowls and shells for salads and desserts.

TACO SHELLS AND CHALUPA SHELLS

Purchased taco shells have about 50 calories and 8 carbohydrate grams. Considering the time involved in trying to prepare your own, I would suggest buying both taco and chalupa shells.

Tortilla Chips

Cut tortillas into 6 or 8 pieces and spread out in a single layer on cookie sheets. Coat both sides with a butter-flavored cooking spray and sprinkle lightly with salt. Bake at 350° for 8 to 10 minutes or until crisp.

Tortilla Strips

Cut tortillas in thirds, then again in very thin strips. Coat the strips with a butter-flavored cooking spray and sprinkle with salt. Bake on cookie sheets at 350° for 5 to 8 minutes or until crisp. Flour tortillas may be toasted in the same way.

Chalupa Shells

Spread corn tortillas in a single layer on a cookie sheet. Coat both sides with a butter-flavored cooking spray and sprinkle lightly with salt. Bake at 350° for 10 to 15 minutes or until crisp.

Tortilla Cups

Like taco shells and chalupa shells, larger corn tortilla shells made to hold salads are now available in most supermarkets. They can be used to hold many different entrée salads.

To make your own, preheat oven to 350°. Coat the tortillas on both sides with a butter-flavored cooking spray. To soften tortillas, place them directly on the oven rack for 1 minute. Remove and shape in one of the following ways:

➡ Press 5- to 6-inch diameter tortillas into muffin containers or 12-ounce custard cups to make small bowls. Bake at 350° until crisp, about 12 minutes.

➡ Press burrito-sized tortillas in large ovenproof bowls to make salad shells for taco salads. Bake 12 to 15 minutes or until crisp. Flour tortillas should be lightly browned.

	Fat	Calories	Carbs
Corn Tortilla (fresh)	1	48	10
Flour Tortilla (6")	2	100	19
Burrito-Sized Flour Tortilla	5–8	150	25
Taco Shell	3–5	50	6–7
Chalupa Shell	3	50	6–7

Check label carefully when buying tortillas for wraps. Fat grams, carbs, and calories vary.

CHICKEN PREPARATION

TO GRILL CHICKEN

To grill chicken to use in salads, soups, or quesadillas, use skinless boneless chicken breast halves. Marinate the chicken breasts for 1 to 2 hours, refrigerated, in the marinade listed in the sidebar.

Preheat the grill to the highest setting. Remove chicken from the marinade and grill over high heat covered until well marked, about 4 minutes. Turn to cook the other side, brushing with marinade at least once. Cook 3 to 4 minutes, covered, and remove. If preparing chicken in advance to be used cold in salads or to be added to soup or quesadillas, seal the cooked chicken tightly in plastic wrap and refrigerate until ready to use. After slicing, season the chicken again with salt and pepper.

Fat grams and calories: The amount of oil absorbed in marinating chicken is minimal—less than one tablespoon per chicken breast.

TO COOK CHICKEN AND PREPARE FOR TACOS, ENCHILADAS, AND FILLINGS

FILLS 10 TACOS OR ENCHILADAS

Chicken will retain more moisture and flavor if cooked on the bone. The pan juices can be added to the final preparation to enhance flavor. If using a purchased roasted chicken, use only the breast and thigh meat. Reserve all juices and add them to the ingredients.

Preheat the oven to 375°.

Clean the chicken and trim away visible fat. Season with salt and pepper. Place in a roasting pan that has been coated with an olive-oil cooking spray. Roast for 20 minutes. Add chicken broth to the pan and continue to cook an additional 10 to 15 minutes, or until chicken is fully cooked.

Marinade
1½ cups safflower oil
½ cup vinegar
3 tablespoons soy sauce
2 jalapeño chiles, chopped
5 cloves garlic, minced
juice from 2 lemons
½ cup chicken broth
½ tablespoon coarsely
    ground black pepper
½ tablespoon sea salt

Seasoned Chicken Filling

5 chicken breast halves, on the bone

salt and pepper to taste

½ cup chicken broth

1 onion, chopped

½ green bell pepper, chopped

1 cup diced tomatoes, or canned tomatoes and green chiles

salt and pepper to taste

½ teaspoon garlic salt

1–2 jalapeño chiles, stemmed, seeded, and diced (optional)

Remove chicken and reserve pan juices. When cool enough to handle, remove the skin and bone, and either shred or cut into small pieces.

Heat a medium skillet over medium heat. Coat generously with a vegetable-oil cooking spray. Add the onion and bell pepper and sauté, stirring a few times to prevent burning. (You may need to add additional spray.) When the onions are soft and lightly browned, add the diced tomatoes and garlic salt and season to taste with salt and pepper. Stir the tomato-onion mixture into the chicken and toss well.

For a spicier filling, stir in the jalapeño chiles.

NUTRITIONAL ANALYIS (PER SERVING, BASED ON 10 SERVINGS)

Calories 155 (19% from fat); Protein 27 grams; Carbohydrates 3 grams; Fiber less than 1 gram; Fat 4 grams.

FAT-FREE STOCK

MAKES ABOUT 2½ CUPS

This flavorful, rich stock has very little fat and is packed with flavor. It takes much less time than you might think and cooks with very little supervision. Use it when cooking beans or as a substitute for chicken broth in enchilada sauces. You may double or triple the recipe if you have a large stock pot.

Trim excess fat from ham hocks and salt pork. Don't worry about leaving some of the fat. You will skim it off later.

Preheat the oven to broil. Coat the onions, garlic, celery, and carrot with a little vegetable-oil cooking spray and place vegetables and chicken wings in a roasting pan on the middle rack. Cook about 8 to 10 minutes, turning several times to brown. Transfer to a large saucepan and add the ham hocks and salt pork. Fill the saucepan with water and chicken broth. Add parsley and bring to a boil. Skim the foam from the top and reduce to a simmer.

Simmer the stock at least 1½ hours or up to 3 hours. Add more water if cooking the maximum time. The longer you cook the stock, the more intense the flavors.

Cool the vegetables in the stock, then strain and discard the bones and vegetables. Refrigerate. Remove solidified fat from the stock and discard.

Store in 1-cup containers or resealable bags.

2 pounds salt pork, fat trimmed

3 smoked ham hocks, fat trimmed

2 large onions, coarsely chopped

6 cloves garlic, coarsely chopped

1 large stalk celery, in pieces

1 large carrot, in pieces

3–6 chicken wings (optional)

6–7 cups water

1 14-ounce can chicken or beef broth

10 parsley sprigs

low-fat, low-carb

meaty bones from a smoked turkey or 2 smoked chickens

2 large onions, coarsely chopped

6 cloves garlic, chopped

2 large stalks celery, coarsely chopped

12 parsley sprigs

2 sprigs fresh thyme

1 tablespoon cracked black pepper

water to cover

Note: Browning the bones under the broiling element of your oven or on an outdoor grill will greatly enhance the flavor of the finished stock. Simply brown on both sides for 6 to 8 minutes.

SMOKED TURKEY STOCK

MAKES ABOUT 2½ TO 3 CUPS

The method for making this stock is similar to that for Fat-Free Stock. The sweetness of the smoked chicken or turkey makes the finished stock particularly good for preparing enchilada sauces made from dried chile pods. I usually make stock in large quantities when I have a smoked turkey and freeze it in 1-cup freezer bags.

Cut a smoked turkey carcass, or 2 smoked chickens, into smaller pieces to easily fit a large stock pot. Put the turkey or chicken pieces, onions, garlic, celery, parsley, thyme, and pepper in the stock pot and fill it with enough water to cover all the bones. Bring to a boil over high heat, skimming the foam from the top.

Reduce the heat and simmer, uncovered, for 2½ to 3 hours. (You may need to add additional water.)

Strain the stock and discard all bones and vegetables. Cool and refrigerate the stock. Remove solidified fat from the stock and discard. Strain the stock again and store in 1 to 2 cup amounts in freezer bags. Do not salt the stock until you use it for cooking. The stock may be frozen for 9 to 12 months.

CORNMEAL CREPES

MAKES 25–28

Crepes made with cornmeal and seasoned with fresh herbs and chiles make a wonderful substitute for corn or flour tortillas. They are easier to roll, and you avoid the oil-drenched method of preparing corn tortillas for enchiladas. When baked with enchilada fillings and sauces, they taste similar to tamales. Crepes do not dry out or get hard like tortillas, have fewer calories, and taste delicious. You may prefer these to corn tortillas. Stacked enchiladas and enchilada casseroles are particularly good when made with cornmeal crepes.

Advance Preparation: Crepes may be prepared a day in advance. They freeze quite well for 3 to 4 months.

Thoroughly mince the chiles (or add the cayenne pepper) and cilantro or parsley in a blender or food processor fitted with the metal blade. Add the egg substitute, water, milk, salt, baking powder, cornmeal, flour, sugar, and oil and blend until very smooth. Let the batter rest at room temperature 30 minutes to an hour.

Heat a well-seasoned crepe pan or small skillet over medium heat. Coat with a vegetable-oil cooking spray. When the pan is hot, add about ¼ cup crepe batter. Tilt the pan, rotating so the batter is evenly distributed. Cook until the crepe appears dry, then turn and cook on the opposite side about 1 minute after. Remove. Spray the pan again and repeat until all the batter has been used.

Store crepes between sheets of wax paper or plastic wrap until ready to use.

½ teaspoon cayenne pepper or 2 serrano chiles, stemmed, seeded

2 sprigs fresh cilantro or parsley

egg substitute equivalent to 4 eggs

1 cup water

1 cup skim milk

1 teaspoon salt

½ teaspoon baking powder

1 cup cornmeal

1 cup all-purpose flour

1 tablespoon sugar

1½ tablespoons safflower oil

NUTRITIONAL ANALYSIS (PER CREPE, BASED ON 25 CREPES PER RECIPE)

Calories 53 (17% from fat); Protein 2 grams; Carbohydrates 9 grams; Fiber less than 1 gram; Fat 1 gram.

1 pound black beans

1 large onion, finely diced

1 large carrot, finely diced

1 celery stalk, finely minced

1 jalapeño chile, stemmed and minced

3 cloves garlic, minced

2 14-ounce cans chicken broth or Fat-Free Stock (p. 13)

¾ cup tomato sauce

3 cups water

3 2–3-ounce chunks smoked pork, all fat trimmed

1–2 teaspoons salt, or to taste

Garnish

Pico de Gallo (p. 28)

light sour cream

Pinto Beans: Cook pinto beans in the same manner. They will take about 30 minutes longer to cook and will require additional water. Nutritional Analysis (per cup, without garnishes): Calories 289 (9% from fat); Protein 18 grams; Carbohydrates 47 grams; Fiber 15 grams; Fat 3 grams.

BLACK BEANS

MAKES ABOUT 6 CUPS

This seems like a lot of vegetables for 1 pound of beans, but they help give the stock good flavor and, if diced quite small, they tend to disappear. If you like the beans very soft or you plan to purée them for soup or a dip, increase the cooking time about 30 minutes.

Soak the beans in enough water to cover for 3 to 4 hours or overnight. Drain and discard the water.

Preheat the oven to 500°. Coat the onion, carrot, celery, and jalapeño with a vegetable-oil cooking spray and place on the center rack. Roast the vegetables about 20 minutes, then turn the setting to "broil" and broil, turning several times, until lightly browned. Remove and cool. Cut into fine dice. (This extra step vastly improves the flavor of the finished product.)

Coat a large saucepan with a vegetable-oil cooking spray and place over medium heat. Add the garlic and sauté, stirring constantly, to release flavor. Add the vegetables and cook until softened, about 5 minutes.

Add the broth or Fat-Free Stock, tomato sauce, water, smoked pork, and beans and bring to a boil. Skim foam from the top, reduce the heat to a simmer, and cook about 1 hour, stirring occasionally. Add salt after the beans are fully cooked. Remove smoked pork and discard. If you want a thicker broth, simply purée about 1 cup of the beans in a blender or food processor and mix them into the remaining beans.

Serve beans with any of the tortilla specialties. Garnish with Pico de Gallo and light sour cream.

**NUTRITIONAL ANALYSIS
(PER CUP, WITHOUT GARNISHES)**

Calories 287 (9% from fat); Protein 20 grams; Carbohydrates 45 grams; Fiber 16 grams; Fat 3 grams.

QUICK BLACK BEANS

MAKES 6 SERVINGS

There are many very acceptable bean products on supermarket shelves—a boon to the increasing number of working cooks! Use the same ingredients and method for pinto beans. This is a good place to use Smoked Turkey Stock (p. 14) or Fat-Free Stock (p. 13).

Advance Preparation: Beans may be prepared a day in advance.

Drain the black beans, reserving all the juices.

Coat a medium saucepan with a vegetable-oil cooking spray and place over medium heat. Add the garlic and onion and sauté until softened. (You may need to use additional spray.) Add the bell pepper and reserved juices from the beans. Simmer about 3 to 4 minutes, then add sausage, chicken or beef broth, and tomato sauce and cook about 10 to 15 minutes. Stir in chiles and beans and cook just long enough to heat thoroughly to make a moderately thick broth. Season to taste with salt and pepper.

2 15-ounce cans black beans, drained

2 cloves garlic, minced

1 cup diced onion

2 tablespoons finely minced bell pepper

1½ ounce low-fat smoked sausage, minced

1 cup chicken or beef broth

¼ cup tomato sauce

2 serrano chiles, stemmed, seeded, and minced

salt and pepper to taste

NUTRITIONAL ANALYSIS (PER CUP)
Calories 174 (10% from fat); Protein 11 grams;
Carbohydrates 27 grams; Fiber 7 grams; Fat 2 grams.

---

1 cup chopped onion

½ teaspoon chili powder

1–2 teaspoons chicken broth
   or water

½ cup low-fat ricotta cheese

½ cup picante sauce

½ teaspoon garlic salt

2 cups cooked pinto or
   black beans (p. 16)

salt and pepper to taste

Garnish

grated cheese

Crema (p. 21)

shredded iceberg lettuce

diced tomatoes

MASHED BEANS

MAKES 4 SERVINGS

Coat a medium skillet generously with a vegetable-oil cooking spray and cook the onion over medium heat, stirring constantly, until lightly browned. Stir in chili powder and 1 to 2 table-spoons chicken broth or water. Remove from heat and transfer to a food processor fitted with the metal blade.

Add the ricotta cheese, picante sauce, garlic salt, and beans. Process to purée. Season to taste with salt and pepper.

If serving beans as a side dish, bring beans to a simmer in a well-seasoned skillet over medium heat and cook until hot and thickened. Serve garnished with grated cheese and Crema, or shredded iceberg lettuce and diced tomatoes.

If using for nachos, spread on toasted tortillas and top with cheese or desired toppings.

NUTRITIONAL ANALYSIS
(PER CUP OF BEANS, NO GARNISH)

Calories 182 (15% from fat); Protein 11 grams;
Carbohydrates 27 grams; Fiber 9 grams; Fat 3 grams.

CILANTRO PESTO

MAKES 1 CUP

Use this to baste grilled fish, chicken, or meats, to season soups, rice, and dips, or wherever you want assertive seasoning.

In a blender or food processor, combine the garlic, parsley, cilantro, oil, pine nuts or almonds, cheese, lemon juice, salt, and pepper until well mixed. Store in a covered container.

BASTING SAUCE

If using as a basting sauce, add 1 cup chicken or beef broth and ½ cup oil.

low-fat, low-carb

4 cloves garlic, peeled

2 cups packed fresh parsley, stemmed

2 cups packed fresh cilantro, stemmed

4 tablespoons safflower oil

2 tablespoons pine nuts or almonds, toasted

1 tablespoon grated Parmesan cheese

1 teaspoon lemon juice

¼ teaspoon salt

pinch white pepper

low-fat, low-carb

5 serrano chiles, stemmed
 and seeded or 1 large
 poblano chile, roasted,
 peeled, seeded

2 cups packed fresh parsley,
 stemmed

2 cups packed fresh cilantro,
 stemmed

5 cloves garlic

2 tablespoons pumpkin
 seeds or pine nuts,
 toasted

1 tablespoon grated
 Parmesan or Romano
 cheese

4 tablespoons safflower oil

squeeze of fresh lime juice

¼–½ teaspoon salt

SPICY GREEN CHILE PESTO

MAKES 1¼ CUPS

You can use this to season rice, top broiled fish, or add to dips when you want to add flavor and spice.

Using a blender or a food processor fitted with the metal blade, process chiles, parsley, cilantro, garlic, and pumpkin seeds or pine nuts. Blend until very finely chopped and combined. Add oil, lime juice, and salt to taste. Process briefly to combine.

Store refrigerated for 2 days or freeze for about 2 months. While the flavors freeze well, the texture becomes somewhat soggy when frozen.

NUTRITIONAL ANALYSIS (PER TABLESPOON)

Calories 43 (74% from fat); Protein less than 1 gram;
Carbohydrates 1 gram; Fiber less than 1 gram; Fat 4 grams.

CREMA

MAKES 2 CUPS

Use this in place of sour cream and save significant fat grams and calories. If you prefer a richer taste, substitute light sour cream for the non-fat sour cream, and you'll still trim the fat. The original crema is made with equal amounts of sour cream and whipping cream with a squeeze of fresh lime juice.

1 cup light sour cream
1 cup plain, low-fat yogurt
¼ cup skim milk
pinch of salt and pepper

Using a whisk, whip the sour cream, yogurt, and skim milk until smooth. Season to taste with salt and pepper.

NUTRITIONAL ANALYSIS (PER TABLESPOON)

Calories 14 (8% from fat); Protein less than 1 gram; Carbohydrates 2 grams; Fiber less than 1 gram; Fat less than 1 gram.

---

1 small clove garlic

½ teaspoon anchovy paste

½ cup packed fresh cilantro
leaves

¼ cup packed fresh parsley
leaves

1 tablespoon vinegar

1 tablespoon lemon juice

2 scallions, mostly the green
part

1½ tablespoons light
mayonnaise

¾ cup light sour cream

salt and pepper to taste

CILANTRO CREAM

MAKES 1⅛ CUPS

Use this sauce as an accent sauce, as a dip for Smoked Salmon Tortilla Bites (p. 65), or with Fish Tacos (p. 142). It is particularly good with grilled salmon.

Put garlic, anchovy paste, cilantro, parsley, vinegar, lemon juice, scallions, and mayonnaise in a blender and blend on high speed to liquefy. Add sour cream and blend to combine. Season with salt and pepper.

Keeps refrigerated for a week.

**NUTRITIONAL ANALYSIS
(PER TABLESPOON)**

Calories 16 (12% from fat); Protein less than 1 gram;
Carbohydrates 2 grams; Fiber less than 1 gram;
Fat less than 1 gram.

BUTTER SAUCES

MAKES 1 CUP

While high in calories and fat, butter sauces have zero carbs, and a small amount goes a long way on grilled or broiled fish. This is a basic preparation that can be varied by adding jalapeño or serrano chiles to the initial reduction, or adding diced tomatoes or sun-dried tomatoes to the final preparation. Do not omit the small amount of cream because it keeps the sauce from breaking. This is best made just prior to serving and kept warm in a double boiler or small thermos.

Using a small saucepan over high heat, bring shallot, vinegar or citrus juice, vermouth or white wine, and serrano chili, if using, to a boil. Boil 2 minutes, then add cream and boil to reduce by about half the original volume. This is the liaison that will bind the butter into a smooth, creamy sauce.

Lift the skillet from the heat and reduce the heat to medium low. Slowly whisk in the butter, 2 to 3 tablespoons at a time, until the sauce is smooth. Remove and strain, then add salt, pepper, and lemon juice to taste. Keep warm atop a double boiler, or warm briefly over low heat and transfer to a thermos until ready to use.

1 shallot, minced

¼ cup vinegar or citrus juice (lemon, lime, or orange)

½ cup vermouth or white wine

1 serrano chili, stemmed, seeded, and halved (optional)

3 tablespoons heavy cream

1½ sticks unsalted butter (6 oz.), cut into tablespoons

salt and white pepper to taste

a few drops lemon juice

NUTRITIONAL ANALYSIS
(PER TABLESPOON
BASED ON 1 CUP PER RECIPE)

Calories 93 (93% from fat); Protein less than 1 gram;
Carbohydrates less than 1 gram; Fiber less than 1 gram;
Fat 9.5 grams.

---

1 clove garlic

10 sprigs fresh parsley or
cilantro

1 tablespoon pickled
jalapeño chili, including
the juice

½ tablespoon lemon juice

⅓ cup water

1 small to medium avocado,
pitted, peeled, and cut
into several pieces

1 cup bottled thick ranch
dressing

salt and pepper to taste

AVOCADO RANCH DRESSING

MAKES 1¾ CUPS

Many bottled ranch dressings found in the refrigerated section at the grocery store are excellent and can be used as a base for Avocado Ranch Dressing or Chipotle Ranch Dressing to use on salads, soft or crispy tacos, chalupas, or as an accent sauce. Recipes using both of these are found throughout the book. The parsley helps preserve the green color.

Put the garlic, parsley or cilantro, and jalapeño in a blender jar. Add lemon juice and blend on high speed to purée. Add water, avocado, and ranch dressing and blend to combine. Add salt and pepper to taste.

Refrigerate until ready to use. This will lose color in 2 days, so it is best to prepare the day you plan to use it.

**NUTRITIONAL ANALYSIS
(PER TABLESPOON)**

Calories 57 (95% from fat); Protein less than 1 gram;
Carbohydrates less than 1 gram; Fiber less than 1 gram;
Fat 6 grams.

CHIPOTLE RANCH DRESSING

MAKE 1½ CUPS

This is a simple dressing packed with flavor and a variety of uses. It has the popular appeal of ranch dressing with a little subtle spice. Many restaurants use chipotle in this way for salads or dipping sauces. It keeps about 10 days.

In a blender, using the on/off switch, combine the chipotle (starting with smaller amount first), red bell pepper, lime juice, and parsley or cilantro. Add half the ranch dressing and process until smooth.

Add remaining dressing, blend just a few seconds, and season to taste with salt. If you want a spicier dressing, add the second teaspoon of chipotle sauce.

Refrigerate until ready to use.

- 1–2 teaspoons canned chipotle, including the sauce
- ½ red bell pepper, roasted and peeled, in several pieces
- 2 teaspoons fresh lime juice
- several sprigs fresh parsley or cilantro
- 1 cup freshly prepared or refrigerated ranch dressing
- salt to taste

**NUTRITIONAL ANALYSIS
(PER TABLESPOON)**

Calories 65 (90% from fat); Protein less than 1 gram;
Carbohydrates less than 1 gram; Fiber less than 1 gram;
Fat 6.5 grams

---

1 tablespoon butter, melted

½ egg white, beaten

2 cups pecan halves

1 tablespoon BBQ spice
(available in spice section)

¼ teaspoon cayenne pepper

½ teaspoon salt

1 package sugar substitute

BBQ PECANS

MAKES 2 CUPS

Use these chopped on salads, whole as a snack, or as a gift for friends.

Preheat oven to 325°.

Coat a cookie sheet (with sides) with a vegetable-oil cooking spray.

Whisk together butter and egg white. Add pecans and toss to coat thoroughly. Discard egg white mixture.

In a separate bowl, combine BBQ spice, cayenne pepper, salt, and sugar substitute. Sprinkle evenly over pecans and toss to coat. Transfer pecans to the prepared cookie sheet and bake about 12 to 15 minutes, or until toasted and crisp.

Store in airtight container.

NUTRITIONAL ANALYSIS
(PER TABLESPOON)
Calories 51 (88% from fat); Protein less than 1 gram;
Carbohydrates 1 gram; Fiber less than 1 gram; Fat 5 grams.

2
Salsas and Dips

Seeing is deceiving. It's eating that's believing.

—James Thurber

Simple table salsas, often called the "salt and pepper" of Southwest food, are equal to catsup in national popularity and retail sales. There are several varieties of picante sauces, some made with fresh tomatoes, others with good-quality canned tomatoes. Flavors are perked up by grilling, roasting, or smoking the tomatoes, and, of course, by adding spicy little chiles. Some salsas are made with a wide variety of fruits, vegetables, and combinations of tomatillos, fruits, corn, and beans. These are almost little salads and make a refreshing contrast to the robust flavors of Southwest dishes. They also add a colorful, non-fat garnish to enchilada plates or quesadillas. Variations are limited only by your imagination and personal taste.

Serve some of the dips with raw vegetable scoops, or use both tortilla chips and vegetable scoops. Many of these salsas can be used as a seasoning. Add them to a simple vinaigrette or butter sauce. Some, such as the Papaya Salsa (p. 36), can be tossed in a grilled chicken salad . . . use your imagination!

6 Roma tomatoes or
   3 medium tomatoes

1 cup diced yellow or white
   onion or 1–2 bunches
   scallions, sliced

3–4 serrano chiles or 1–3
   jalapeño chiles, stemmed,
   seeded, and finely diced

juice from 1 lime

1 tablespoon light olive oil

salt and white pepper to
   taste

1 tablespoon minced fresh
   cilantro

PICO DE GALLO

MAKES ABOUT 4 CUPS, 8 SERVINGS

You can adjust the amount and type of heat in this fresh salsa by the kind and amount of chile used. Serrano chiles produce a somewhat subtle "late" heat, while jalapeños give that forward "lip-searing" heat. Removing both seeds and membrane lessens the heat. This is a good basic salsa from which you can make many variations. I prefer using either Roma tomatoes, cherry tomatoes, or a combination of red and yellow teardrop tomatoes because they have better flavor.

Remove cores from tomatoes and cut evenly into ¼-inch dice. Place in a glass bowl.

In a strainer, rinse onion under ice cold water to remove bitter liquids. Add to the tomatoes along with chiles, lime juice, and olive oil. Season to taste with salt, pepper, and cilantro.

Refrigerate 2 hours before using.

> **NUTRITIONAL ANALYSIS (PER ½-CUP)**
> Calories 41 (39% from fat); Protein less than 1 gram;
> Carbohydrates 4 grams; Fiber 1 gram; Fat 2 grams.

Avocado Salsa: Add 1 avocado peeled, cored, and diced, with additional lime juice, salt, and cilantro. Nutritional Analysis (per ⅔-cup): Calories 78 (57% from fat); Protein 1 gram; Carbohydrates 6 grams; Fiber 2 grams; Fat 5 grams.

Black Bean Salsa: Add 1 cup well-seasoned, cooked black beans and ¾ cup mango or papaya. Adjust seasonings by adding more lime juice and salt. Nutritional Analysis (per ¾-cup): Calories 74 (21% from fat); Protein 3 grams; Carbohydrates 10 grams; Fiber 3 grams; Fat 2 grams.

California Salsa: Add ½ cup each diced black and green olives and ½ cup toasted pumpkin seeds. Use scallions in place of white or yellow onions. Nutritional Analysis (per ⅔-cup): Calories 98 (68% from fat); Protein 3 grams; Carbohydrates 5 grams; Fiber 1 gram; Fat 7.5 grams.

GRILLED CORN AND PEPPER SALSA

MAKES 3½ CUPS, SERVES 6

Preheat an indoor or outdoor grill to the highest setting (or use the broiling element of your oven).

Generously coat the corn with a vegetable-oil cooking spray and sprinkle lightly with chili powder, salt, and pepper. Grill or broil on both sides 4 to 5 minutes. Using a sharp knife, cut corn kernels from the cob. Set aside.

Generously coat a medium skillet with vegetable-oil cooking spray and place over medium heat. Add the onion and sauté 1 to 2 minutes. Do not brown.

Combine onion, corn, bell peppers, and serrano chiles in a small bowl. Season with lime juice, salt, and pepper.

4 ears fresh corn, shucked

chili powder

salt and pepper

1 cup diced red onion

1–2 teaspoons safflower oil

1 green bell pepper, stemmed, seeded, and diced

1 red bell pepper, stemmed, seeded, and diced

2 serrano chiles, diced

fresh lime juice

salt and pepper to taste

NUTRITIONAL ANALYSIS (PER ½-CUP)

Calories 90 (23% from fat); Protein 3 grams;
Carbohydrates 14 grams; Fiber 4 grams; Fat 2.5 grams.

4–5 large, vine-ripe
  tomatoes, cores intact

safflower oil

2–3 serrano chiles, stemmed

2 tablespoons minced fresh
  cilantro

salt and white pepper to
  taste

lime juice to taste

GRILLED TOMATO SALSA

SERVES 8

This is my favorite table salsa that I learned to make from my good friend Jesse Calvillo. Smoking the tomatoes prior to grilling greatly enhances their flavor.

Preheat the oven to 300°.

Rub tomatoes with oil and place on an outdoor grill over high heat. Cover the grill and cook the tomatoes until they are lightly charred and the juices begin to flow, about 10 to 12 minutes. Turn tomatoes to expose all sides.

Remove tomatoes. Cut in half and place on an oiled cookie sheet. Roast in the oven 15 to 20 minutes or until very soft.

Put tomatoes and their juices in a blender with serrano chiles and blend until smooth. (You will have to do this in several batches.) Season with cilantro, salt, pepper, and lime juice.

NUTRITIONAL ANALYSIS (PER ¼-CUP)

Calories 9 (9% from fat); Protein less than 1 gram;
Carbohydrates 1 gram; Fiber less than 1 gram;
Fat less than 1 gram.

Note: If the salsa congeals, add 1 to 2 tablespoons vinegar and simmer over medium-low heat for 5 to 8 minutes. When tomatoes are not ripe, the salsa will not have a rich, red color. In this case, add 1 cup canned puréed tomatoes including juices.

TOMATO AND GREEN CHILE SALSA

SERVES 8

This quick salsa is a good choice in winter months when ripe tomatoes are scarce.

Coat a medium skillet with a nonstick vegetable-oil cooking spray and place over medium heat. Add garlic and onion and sauté a few seconds. The idea is to cook the onions and garlic enough to release their flavor but keep them slightly crisp.

Add the green chiles to the onion mixture. Remove from the heat.

Using a blender or a food processor fitted with the metal blade, blend the tomatoes to purée. Combine tomatoes, green chiles and onion mixture, jalapeños, and vinegar in a mixing bowl. Season to taste with salt, pepper, and cilantro. Store refrigerated.

low-fat, low-carb

1 clove garlic, minced

1 medium yellow onion, diced

1 4½-ounce can green chiles

1 16-ounce can tomatoes

2–4 fresh jalapeño chiles, seeded, stemmed, and diced

1 tablespoon red wine vinegar

salt and pepper to taste

1 tablespoon minced fresh cilantro

NUTRITIONAL ANALYSIS (PER ¼-CUP)

Calories 12 (6% from fat); Protein Less than 1 gram;
Carbohydrates 2 grams; Fiber less than 1 gram;
Fat less than 1 gram

1–2 jalapeño chiles, stemmed and seeded

½–1 bunch cilantro, stemmed and washed

1 28-ounce can diced tomatoes, including the juices

juice from one lime

2 tablespoons light olive oil

1 envelope zesty Italian dressing mix

QUICK WINTER SALSA

MAKES 3¾ CUPS

One of my good friends, Karen Harlan, claims this is the only recipe anyone asks her for. While I doubt that, it is an excellent salsa when ripe tomatoes are not available or when you are in a hurry. You can use as much or as little cilantro as you like, and you may vary the heat by using more or less jalapeño. Do not use a blender or the mixture turns pink and foamy.

Using a food processor fitted with the metal blade, start the machine running and drop chiles and cilantro through the feed tube. Process to mince. Add tomatoes, lime juice, olive oil, and dressing mix. Process to combine.

Store in a glass container. Keeps about one week.

NUTRITIONAL ANALYSIS
(PER ¼ CUP)
Calories 33 (54% from fat); Protein less than 1 gram;
Carbohydrates 4 grams; Fiber less than 1 gram;
Fat 2 grams.

CHIPOTLE SALSA

Add 2 tablespoons of orange juice and 2 tablespoons of adobo sauce from canned chipotle chiles.

NUTRITIONAL ANALYSIS
(PER 2 TABLESPOONS)
Calories 17 (53% from fat); Protein less than 1 gram;
Carbohydrates 2 grams; Fiber less than 1 gram;
Fat less than 1 gram.

GREEN CHILE SALSA

MAKES 2½-3 CUPS, SERVES 8

This salsa is best when made with New Mexico green chiles. They are hotter than California Anaheim chiles and truly "set your heart and soul on fire." Try serving 3 or 4 salsas with toasted tortillas the next time you entertain guests. You'll find it fun to "mix and match." This is a very flavorful salsa, almost zero carbs. See the note at the end of the recipe to make a sauce for a breakfast omelette. Serve this salsa warm or at room temperature.

Heat a medium skillet over medium-high heat. Put the pork in the hot pan and sear, without stirring, until browned and juices no longer run red. When browned, break up the pork with a fork and add garlic and onion. Sauté until pork is fully cooked and onions are translucent. Season with salt and pepper.

Add chiles to the pork and onion mixture. Balance the flavors by adding vinegar and a pinch of sugar. Taste and adjust seasonings.

Serve with toasted tortilla chips.

NUTRITIONAL ANALYSIS
(PER ⅓-CUP, BASED ON 3-CUP RECIPE)
Calories 55 (26% from fat); Protein 6 grams;
Carbohydrates 4 grams; Fiber 1 gram; Fat 1.5 grams.

¼ pound ground pork

2 cloves garlic, minced

1 onion, chopped

1–1½ teaspoons salt

pinch white pepper

15–16 fresh green chiles (about 1 pound), roasted, peeled, and diced ¼ inch, or 4 4½-ounce cans diced green chiles

½ cup canned diced tomatoes

2 teaspoons to 1 tablespoon cider vinegar

pinch sugar (if needed)

Note: To make a sauce for an omelette, thin the salsa with a rich chicken broth, using enough to make a sauce consistency. Add ½ cup (canned) diced tomatoes and cook 3 to 4 minutes and serve on a simple cheese omelette. If you can, buy Hatch green chiles, canned or frozen. They are the best.

½ cup packed cilantro leaves

14 tomatillos, husks removed, rinsed, and quartered

2 serrano chiles, stemmed and seeded

2–3 pieces of ripe mango, papaya, or cantaloupe, about 1-inch square

1 clove garlic, minced

2 shallots, minced

2 tablespoons white wine

2 teaspoons fresh lime juice

salt to taste

pinch white pepper

TOMATILLO SALSA

SERVES 6

Tomatillos have a slightly tart, citrus flavor. This is a very refreshing salsa that is particularly good with chicken or grilled salmon. Tomatillos, like lemons, vary in acidity. Adding some fruit helps balance any bitterness.

Using a blender or food processor fitted with the metal blade, process the cilantro, tomatillos, chiles, and fruit until well blended. If using a blender, use on/off turns to prevent liquefying. You may need to do this in several batches.

Put the garlic and shallot in a small saucepan with the white wine and bring to a boil over medium heat to "sweat." Cool and blend with the tomatillos.

Season to taste with lime juice, salt, and white pepper. Refrigerate until ready to use.

NUTRITIONAL ANALYSIS (PER SERVING)
Calories 48 (16% from fat); Protein 1 gram;
Carbohydrates 9 grams; Fiber 2 grams; Fat less than 1 gram.

MANGO SALSA

SERVES 6

This is a refreshing summer salsa that is good with grilled chicken or fish and as a garnish for soft tacos. I particularly like it with Chicken Margarita (page 124). If you cannot find good mangoes, substitute ripe papayas.

Use firm, but ripe mango. Over-ripe fruits are difficult to dice because they turn to mush.

Put the onion in a shallow dish and cover with vinegar and ice water. Soak for 30 minutes. Strain.

In a glass bowl, gently combine the mango, onions, peppers, and chiles. Season to taste with lime juice, olive oil, salt, and cilantro. Refrigerate for 1 hour before serving.

1½ cups diced mango

1 cup diced red onion

2 tablespoons rice wine vinegar

ice water

1 cup roasted, peeled, and diced red bell pepper

2 serrano chiles, stemmed, seeded, and diced

1–2 teaspoons fresh lime juice

1 tablespoon light olive oil or safflower oil

salt to taste

1 tablespoon minced fresh cilantro

NUTRITIONAL ANALYSIS (PER SERVING)

Calories 52 (3% from fat); Protein less than 1 gram;
Carbohydrates 11 grams; Fiber 1 gram; Fat less than 1 gram.

½ cup diced fresh pineapple

1 small papaya, peeled, seeded, and diced

1½ cups diced fresh tomatoes

a few drops light olive oil

2–3 serrano chiles, seeded, stemmed, and diced

1 cup finely diced red onion

½ cup finely diced red bell pepper

juice from 1 lime

salt and white pepper to taste

1 teaspoon minced fresh basil or mint

PAPAYA SALSA

SERVES 6

Chiles marry well with fruits; they actually intensify the fruit flavor. This salsa is very mild and goes well with pork, poultry, or breakfast tacos.

Dice the pineapple and papaya in ⅛- to ¼-inch dice.

Mix pineapple, papaya, tomatoes, and oil with serrano chiles in a glass bowl.

Add the onion and bell pepper to the pineapple. Season with lime, salt, pepper, and basil or mint. Refrigerate 1 to 2 hours before using.

NUTRITIONAL ANALYSIS (PER SERVING)
Calories 50 (12% from fat); Protein 1 gram;
Carbohydrates 10 grams; Fiber 2 grams; Fat less than 1 gram.

SUMMER MELON SALSA

SERVES 8

This is a colorful, slightly spicy salsa that is excellent with grilled fish or poultry. Choose melons that are ripe but firm and dice them in even, ¼-inch squares.

Combine cucumber, melon, pepper, chiles, vinegar, and basil or cilantro in a glass bowl and season to taste with salt and pepper. Refrigerate 1 to 2 hours before serving.

NUTRITIONAL ANALYSIS (PER SERVING)

Calories 28 (3% from fat); Protein less than 1 gram;
Carbohydrates 5 grams; Fiber less than 1 gram;
Fat less than 1 gram.

---

1 cup diced cucumber

1 cup diced cantaloupe melon

1 cup diced honeydew melon

½ cup diced red bell pepper

2 serrano chiles, seeded, stemmed, and minced

1 tablespoon rice wine vinegar

1 tablespoon minced basil or cilantro

salt and white pepper to taste

low-fat, low-carb

½ cup diced red onion

¼ cup white wine vinegar

ice water

8 tomatillos, husks removed, rinsed, and diced ¼ inch

1 pint yellow cherry tomatoes, diced ¼ inch

4 Roma tomatoes, diced ¼ inch

1–2 serrano chiles, stemmed, seeded, and minced

1–2 teaspoons fresh lime juice

1 tablespoon safflower oil

salt to taste

1 tablespoon minced fresh basil or cilantro

THREE TOMATO SALSA
SERVES 6

This is a colorful Pico de Gallo–type salsa that is very mild. Use it with grilled fish, on salads, or with fajitas and quesadillas.

Soak the onion in vinegar and ice water to cover for 30 minutes. Drain and toss with tomatillos, tomatoes, and serrano chiles.

Season to taste with fresh lime juice, safflower oil, salt, and basil or cilantro. Refrigerate at least 1 hour before using.

NUTRITIONAL ANALYSIS (PER SERVING)

Calories 50 (14% from fat); Protein 1 gram;
Carbohydrates 8 grams; Fiber 2 grams; Fat less than 1 gram.

JICAMA SALSA

SERVES 6

When these ingredients are diced, the result is a Pico de Gallo–type salsa. If cut into julienne strips, they make an attractive little salad that can be used to garnish tortilla specialties.

Thinly slice jicama and then cut into a ¼-inch dice. Core and seed peppers and cut into ¼-inch dice.

Blanch the carrot until you can pierce it with a fork, then rinse under cool water and dice ½ inch.

Combine jicama, peppers, and carrot and toss with lime juice, vinegar, salt, pepper, and cilantro. Refrigerate several hours before using.

½ small jicama, peeled
1 red bell pepper
1 yellow bell pepper
1 green bell pepper
1 carrot, peeled
juice from ½ lime
1 tablespoon rice wine
   vinegar
salt and pepper to taste
minced fresh cilantro

NUTRITIONAL ANALYSIS (PER SERVING):
Calories 23 (4% from fat); Protein less than 1 gram;
Carbohydrates 5 grams; Fiber 2 grams; Fat less than 1 gram.

1 tomatillo, husk removed, rinsed, and quartered

6–8 sprigs parsley or cilantro

3 poblano chiles, roasted, peeled, and seeded

3 ounces light or low-fat cream cheese

2–3 tablespoons chicken broth (if needed)

2 tablespoons warm safflower oil

fresh lime juice to taste

½ teaspoon garlic salt

salt to taste

CHILE POBLANO CREAM

MAKES 1½ CUPS

This spicy cream may be used as a dip or drizzled on beans, chalupas, soups, or tacos for a little spice.

Using a blender, blend the tomatillos with parsley or cilantro and chiles until smooth.

Add cream cheese in several pieces and blend smooth. You may need to add chicken broth to aid blending.

Heat the safflower oil and add it with the blender running to help emulsify the mixture. Season with lime juice and garlic salt. Add additional salt if desired.

Store in the refrigerator until ready to use. The cream keeps well for 3 to 4 days. Reblend before using if necessary.

**NUTRITIONAL ANALYSIS
(PER TABLESPOON)**

Calories 26 (74% from fat); Protein less than 1 gram;
Carbohydrates 1 gram; Fiber less than 1 gram; Fat 2 grams.

QUESO

MAKES ABOUT 2¾ CUPS

This simple traditional recipe makes a better Queso than any purchased brand that I have tried and has many uses.

➡ Drizzle over steamed vegetables.

➡ Serve with chips or raw vegetables such as celery, broccoli, carrots, or cauliflower.

➡ Serve with tacos in place of grated cheese.

➡ Thin with a small amount of water or chicken broth and use as a sauce.

Put diced onion in a small saucepan with water and place over medium-high heat. Bring to a boil and simmer for a minute. Add green chiles and tomatoes and cook about 5 minutes.

Reduce the heat to medium and add cheese in several batches. Stir constantly until the cheese is melted.

Can be kept refrigerated about one week. Reheat in a microwave oven.

½–¾ cup diced onion

2 tablespoons water

2 tablespoons diced green chiles

5–10 ounces canned tomatoes and green chiles (use greater amount for a thinner Queso)

16 ounces light American processed cheese (such as Velveeta), cut into small pieces

---

NUTRITIONAL ANALYSIS
(PER 2 TABLESPOONS)

Calories 66 (27% from fat); Protein 4 grams;
Carbohydrates 3 grams; Fiber less than 1 gram; Fat 2 grams.

---

2 small poblano chiles,
  roasted and peeled

4 ounces Manchego cheese,
  cut into small pieces

4 ounces Havarti cheese,
  cut into small pieces

3 ounces light or low-fat
  cream cheese

2 tablespoons safflower or
  light olive oil

¼ cup water

½ cup diced onion

salt to taste

⅓ cup fresh diced tomatoes
  (optional)

QUESO WITH RAJAS

MAKES 2 CUPS

Many cooks have an aversion to processed cheese. This method uses Mexican cheeses, emulsified using a food processor. Do not omit the oil, as it aids the process. This makes a delicious sauce.

Tomatoes are optional. I like them for the flavor, but they do give the Queso an orange color. The texture is a little thinner than most Queso recipes.

Cut the poblano chile into 4 to 5 pieces.

Using a food processor fitted with the metal blade, process Manchego and Havarti cheese until very finely chopped. Add cream cheese and process to combine.

With the machine running, add the oil through the feed tube and process until very well combined. Add poblano chile and pulse to chop and combine. Set aside.

In a small saucepan, bring water and onion to a boil. Reduce the heat and simmer until onion is softened, about 2 minutes. Over low heat, add the cheese mixture, in batches, until completely melted and smooth. Season to taste with salt.

If adding tomatoes, stir them into final cheese mixture. The Queso will thicken as it cools.

**NUTRITIONAL ANALYSIS
(PER 2 TABLEPSOONS)**
Calories 83 (70% from fat); Protein 4 grams;
Carbohydrates 2 grams; Fiber less than 1 gram; Fat 6.5 grams.

SOUTHWEST SPINACH DIP

SERVES A CROWD

I first had this dip at a neighborhood party and it was so popular it disappeared after about 30 minutes. When everyone asked for the recipe, Claudia and Katy Nelson were kind enough to share it. I spread a very light layer of sour cream and fresh minced parsley on top to enhance the presentation. Serve it with tortilla chips and vegetable scoops. My tasters liked it cold as well as heated.

Preheat the oven to 350°.

Using a mixing bowl, cream together the cream cheese, grated cheese and sour cream until well mixed. Stir in the remaining ingredients and transfer to an ovenproof 1½-quart casserole.

Heat, covered for 20 minutes, then uncover and continue cooking 10 more minutes.

After 5 minutes, spread lightly with sour cream and mined parsley. Serve with tortilla chips and vegetable scoops.

low-fat, low-carb

8 ounces light cream cheese, at room temperature

8–10 ounces grated cheese (Monterey jack, Havarti, Manchego or a low-fat cheddar)

½ cup light sour cream

1 can (original) Ro*tel tomatoes and green chiles, drained

1 can Hot Ro*tel tomatoes and green chiles, undrained

1 10-ounce box chopped frozen spinach, thawed and drained

¼ cup diced and seeded jalapeno chiles (bottled)

½ cup chopped onion

2 small tomatillos, husks removed, rinsed, and quartered

1 clove garlic

¼ cup diced green chiles

3 sprigs cilantro or parsley

1 avocado, peeled, pitted, and cut into several pieces

3 tablespoons light or non-fat sour cream

salt and pepper to taste

fresh lemon juice (optional)

¼ cup diced onion or scallions

⅓ cup diced fresh tomatoes

SKINNY GUACAMOLE

MAKES 4 SERVINGS

This is a chunky-style guacamole that extends one avocado and helps reduce fat and calories. For best results, buy avocados 2 or 3 days before using and let them ripen away from direct sunlight. Light sour cream, non-fat sour cream, and light or low-fat cream cheese all work well in this recipe. If you don't mind a few extra calories, use two avocados and add a little fresh lemon juice. The tomatillos help keep the color fresh.

Using a blender or food processor, process the tomatillos with garlic, chiles, and cilantro or parsley to purée. Add the avocado and sour cream, processing just enough to combine. Season to taste with salt, pepper, and fresh lemon juice.

Rinse the onion or scallions with cold water to remove any bitter liquids. Stir in onion and tomatoes by hand.

When serving this as a salad or accompaniment to tortilla specialties, place a toasted tortilla chip in the center of the guacamole for garnish.

NUTRITIONAL ANALYSIS (PER SERVING)
Calories 108 (72% from fat); Protein 2 grams;
Carbohydrates 6 grams; Fiber 4 grams; Fat 9 grams.

SHRIMP DIP

MAKES ABOUT 4 CUPS, SERVES 8 TO 10

My friend Luann Sewell serves a dip very similar to this, which is very popular (hence the origin of this recipe). It is a great emergency appetizer, as most of the ingredients are ones we usually have on hand. You can double this for a large party.

Preheat the oven to 350°.

Using a food processor fitted with the metal blade, process parsley and almonds until finely minced. Set aside.

Without washing the bowl, use the same bowl and blade and process the shrimp until minced. Add cream cheese, smoked Gouda, mayonnaise, oil, garlic powder, and cayenne pepper and process until light and fluffy. Add onion and pulse a few times to incorporate.

Transfer to a 1-quart ovenproof dish and top with almond/parsley crumbs. Coat lightly with olive oil or butter-flavored cooking spray. Bake about 30 minutes, or until lightly browned and bubbly. If the top browns too quickly, cover it with foil. Serve with low-fat crackers or colorful bell pepper and celery scoops.

1 cup fresh parsley leaves

¼ cup whole almonds

1 6-ounce can cocktail shrimp, drained

12 ounces light or low-fat cream cheese

1½ ounces smoked Gouda cheese, in pieces

2 tablespoons mayonnaise

1 tablespoon safflower oil

½ teaspoon garlic powder

pinch cayenne pepper

½ cup chopped onion

NUTRITIONAL ANALYSIS (PER ½-CUP)

Calories 214 (68% from fat); Protein 12 grams;
Carbohydrates 6 grams; Fiber less than 1 gram; Fat 16 grams.

1 15-ounce can ranch style black beans

¼ teaspoon cumin

¼ teaspoon garlic salt

2½–3 cups diced, cooked chicken breast (from a purchased roasted chicken)

reserved juices from the chicken

salt and pepper

6 ounces crumbled goat cheese or Cotija cheese

1¼ cups Pico de Gallo (in refrigerated section of most supermarkets or p. 28)

Note: If you have Cilantro Pesto (p. 19) or a basil pesto on hand, stir 1 to 2 tablespoons into the Pico de Gallo. Great flavor.

QUICK BLACK BEAN AND CHICKEN DIP

SERVES 12

This is a good recipe to bring to a party when asked to bring something. All the ingredients can be purchased so all you have to do is assemble the dip.

Advance Preparation: If making this in advance, you do not have to remove any liquid from the beans. Prepare as directed, then cover and refrigerate until ready to heat and serve. Reheat in a 350° oven for about 15 to 20 minutes, then top with Pico de Gallo and serve.

Preheat oven to 350°.

Remove about 2 tablespoons liquid from the ranch style beans. Stir cumin and garlic salt into the beans. Place the beans in a medium skillet over medium-high heat and bring to a simmer. Using a fork, mash the beans. Many will remain whole, but this does thicken the mixture. Transfer to an 8 × 8 × 2 casserole dish or 8-inch round dish.

Remove chicken from the bone and dice. Reserve all juices and toss with the chicken. Season with salt and pepper. Put the seasoned chicken on top of the beans. Top evenly with crumbled cheese.

Before serving, heat covered for about 15 to 25 minutes or until hot. Top immediately with Pico de Gallo. Serve with tortilla chips or low-carb crackers.

NUTRITIONAL ANALYSIS (PER SERVING)
Calories 150 (33% from fat); Protein 15 grams;
Carbohydrates 10 grams; Fiber 4 grams; Fat 5.5 grams.

3
Appetizers and Snacks

There is no love sincerer than the love of food.
—George Bernard Shaw

In Mexico, antojitos (snacks) are served as appetizers and are primarily tortilla or masa based. At some tables, partaking of these snacks can go on for hours and is followed by a late-evening meal. While imitating this tradition is not recommended for a low-fat lifestyle, antojitos for a party or for an afternoon of football are a sure winner.

The many varieties of quesadillas are surprisingly low in calories and carbs, and fun to serve with different salsas. Southwest Party Dip (p. 49) is a lightened version of the popular layered dip made with beans, guacamole, and cheese, but this one is lower in both fat and calories. Some dips have more fat than others, but all have been reduced in calories, carbs, and fat. You can always serve dips with vegetable scoops or low-carb crackers in place of tortilla chips.

The many varied ceviche and shrimp cocktail recipes score low in all three categories (fat, calories, and carbs) as do the Tortilla Bites (p. 65) and Anticuchos (p. 51).

1 pound top round, ground

2 cloves garlic, minced

4 teaspoons chili powder

½ cup diced green bell
    pepper

½ cup diced red bell pepper

1 onion, diced

½ teaspoon salt

¼ teaspoon coarsely ground
    black pepper

½ teaspoon red chile flakes

1½ cups stone-ground
    cornmeal

½ cup all-purpose flour

1 tablespoon sugar

4 teaspoons baking powder

egg substitute equivalent to
    2 eggs

¾ cup milk

2 cups canned creamed corn

2 teaspoons salt

2 jalapeño chiles, minced

4 ounces low-fat cheddar
    cheese, grated

2 tablespoons grated
    Parmesan cheese

Variation: Fat grams and calories may be cut further by using ground turkey in place of beef or by substituting a low-fat commercial chili (without beans) for the beef mixture for a "quick" version. In this case, if the chili has a moderately thin sauce, stir 1 to 2 tablespoons cornmeal into the warm chili to thicken.

CHILE CORNBREAD SQUARES

MAKES 24 APPETIZER SQUARES

MAKES 8 ENTRÉE SERVINGS

This variation on a tamale pie is a good addition to a buffet table or a tasty contribution when you have offered to "bring something." Great for tailgate parties or hearty appetizers.

Preheat the oven to 350°.

In a medium skillet, over medium heat, sauté the ground beef and garlic until lightly browned. Add the chili powder and stir to coat all the meat. Add the bell pepper, onion, salt, pepper, and chile flakes and cook, stirring occasionally, about 5 minutes. Remove and set aside.

Combine cornmeal, flour, sugar, and baking powder in a bowl and mix well.

In a separate mixing bowl, beat the egg substitute with milk, creamed corn, salt, and chiles. Combine with the cornmeal mixture and mix well.

Coat a 9 × 13 casserole with a butter-flavored cooking spray. Pour about two-thirds of the batter into the pan. Bake 5 minutes, then remove and sprinkle evenly with the cheddar cheese. Top with the meat mixture, the remaining batter, and Parmesan cheese.

Bake for 40 to 45 minutes or until cornbread tests done. Cool about 10 minutes before cutting into squares.

NUTRITIONAL ANALYSIS (PER APPETIZER)

Calories 115 (22% from fat); Protein 9 grams;
Carbohydrates 14 grams; Fiber 1 gram; Fat 3 grams.

SOUTHWEST PARTY DIP

SERVES 10

The ingredients in most versions of this popular dip can add up to a staggering amount of calories. In this recipe, calories and fat are trimmed from each layer, and the amount of cheese is minimized.

Coat a medium skillet generously with a vegetable-oil cooking spray. Add the beef. Sear on medium-high heat until browned. Add garlic, onion, bell pepper, chili powder, and chiles. Sauté, tossing constantly, 3 to 4 minutes.

Add the pinto beans and cream cheese. Cook 2 to 3 minutes or until combined. Transfer the mixture to a food processor fitted with the metal blade, add picante sauce, and process until puréed. Season with salt and pepper. Spoon the beans into an 8-inch round plate.

Put half the grated cheese on top of the beans. Add guacamole on top of the cheese. Put remaining cheese around the edges, allowing the guacamole to be visible in the center. Arrange the tomatoes inside the cheese.

Garnish with diced chiles and serve with Toasted Tortilla Chips.

¼ pound lean ground beef

2 cloves garlic minced

1 onion, chopped

¼ cup minced green bell pepper

1½ teaspoons chili powder

1 jalapeño chile, stemmed, seeded, and minced

¼ cup diced green chiles

1 16-ounce can pinto beans

4 tablespoons light or low-fat cream cheese

2–3 tablespoons picante sauce

salt and pepper to taste

4 ounces low-fat cheddar cheese, grated

Skinny Guacamole (p. 44)

¾ cup diced tomatoes

Garnish

1 jalapeño chile, fresh or pickled, finely diced

Toasted Tortilla Chips (p. 9)

NUTRITIONAL ANALYSIS
(PER SERVING, WITHOUT GARNISH)

Calories 151 (41% from fat); Protein 9 grams;
Carbohydrates 13 grams; Fiber 4 grams; Fat 7 grams.

---

2 skinless boneless chicken
    breast halves, cooked

chicken stock

salt and pepper

12 corn tortillas

butter-flavored cooking
    spray

salt

4 cups thinly sliced leaf
    lettuce

Garnishes

Skinny Guacamole (p. 44)

1 cup diced tomatoes

Chile Poblano Cream
    (p. 40)

picante sauce

FLAUTAS

SERVES 4

Flautas are crisp little rolled tacos, sometimes called "taquitos," which
are filled with beef or chicken and are usually fried. Soft or crisp, flautas make wonderful little appetizers. Use very thin corn tortillas for
flautas and bake them instead of frying to reduce fat calories.

Shred the chicken meat and moisten with a small amount of
chicken stock. Season with salt and pepper.

One at a time, microwave tortillas on high for 15 seconds to
soften. Place about 1½ tablespoons shredded chicken in the center of each one. Roll up tightly in a cigar shape and seal with two
toothpicks.

Coat rolled tortillas on all sides with a butter-flavored cooking spray, sprinkle with salt, and place seam side down on a
baking dish. Bake in a preheated 375° oven until crisp, about 20
minutes.

Serve flautas on a bed of thinly sliced lettuce with Skinny
Guacamole and diced tomatoes, or arrange on a serving tray with
Chile Poblano Cream and picante sauce for dipping.

**NUTRITIONAL ANALYSIS
(PER FLAUTA, WITHOUT GARNISH)**
Calories 105 (14% from fat); Protein 10 grams;
Carbohydrates 11 grams; Fiber 1 gram; Fat 1.5 grams.

ANTICUCHOS

MAKES 12 SKEWERS EACH, OF CHICKEN, SHRIMP, AND SWORDFISH

Anticuchos are skewered pieces of beef, chicken, or shrimp that are marinated and grilled. These are fun to serve at a backyard barbecue with a variety of salsas. If preparing beef anticuchos, use beef tenderloin. No marinade is necessary.

To make the marinade, put the garlic, serrano chiles, and cilantro in a blender jar and blend until diced. You may need to add some of the lime juice to aid blending. Remove and combine with remaining lime juice, olive oil, wine, salt, and chile flakes in a shallow bowl. Divide the marinade, using two-thirds for the shrimp and swordfish, one-third for the chicken.

To make the anticuchos, soak the skewers in hot water for 1 hour.

Trim fat from the chicken and cut into ¾-inch square pieces. Remove skin and black portion of swordfish and cut into ¾-inch pieces. Marinate shrimp and swordfish together, chicken separately, for 1 to 1½ hours. Remove and skewer chicken, shrimp, and swordfish on separate skewers.

Preheat an outdoor grill with a hot fire. Remove skewered meats from the marinade and place on the grill. Season with salt and pepper and grill on both sides for about 5 minutes. Brush at least once with the marinade.

Serve Anticuchos with Chile Poblano Cream, Grilled Tomato Salsa, or Chipotle Ranch Dressing.

Marinade

2 garlic cloves

3 serrano chiles, stemmed and seeded

1 cup packed cilantro leaves

1 cup fresh lime juice

2 cups olive oil

½ cup white wine

2 teaspoons coarse salt

1½ tablespoons red chile flakes

Anticuchos

wooden skewers

3 skinless and boneless chicken breast halves

1 pound shrimp, peeled, tails intact

10 ounces swordfish

salt and pepper

Sauces

Chile Poblano Cream (p. 40)

Grilled Tomato Salsa (p. 30)

Cilantro Cream (p. 22)

Chipotle Ranch Dressing (p. 25)

NUTRITIONAL ANALYSIS (PER CHICKEN SKEWER, WITHOUT SAUCES)
Calories 129 (52% from fat); Protein 14 grams;
Carbohydrates less than 1 gram; Fiber less than 1 gram; Fat 7.5 grams.

NUTRITIONAL ANALYSIS (PER SHRIMP SKEWER, WITHOUT SAUCES)
Calories 98 (59% from fat); Protein 9 grams;
Carbohydrates 1 gram; Fiber less than 1 gram; Fat 6.5 grams.

NUTRITIONAL ANALYSIS (PER SWORDFISH SKEWER, WITHOUT SAUCES)
Calories 87 (72% from fat); Protein 5 grams;
Carbohydrates less than 1 gram; Fiber less than 1 gram; Fat 7 grams.

3 cups water

2 cups vermouth or white wine

3–4 slices white onion

1 pound large sea scallops

½ pound salmon fillets

2 cups fresh lemon juice

⅓ cup fresh orange juice

⅓ cup fresh lime juice

2 serrano chiles, stemmed, seeded, and minced

3 tablespoons light olive oil, divided use

2 tablespoons fresh minced cilantro

1 cup diced tomato

4 tablespoons diced red onion

2 tablespoons fresh orange juice

¼ cup fresh lime juice

½ teaspoon salt

¼ teaspoon white pepper

½ avocado, diced (optional)

SCALLOP AND SALMON CEVICHE
SERVES 6

This ceviche is very colorful and appetizing. It is not necessary to poach the salmon, providing it is fresh (not fresh frozen). Do not be overwhelmed by the number of ingredients—this is very simple once you have assembled your ingredients and is well worth the effort.

In a medium sauce pan, bring water and white wine or vermouth to a rolling boil. Add the scallops and onion, cover, then remove from heat and let stand 5 minutes. Remove scallops and cool. Cut into bite-sized pieces.

Using a sharp knife, cut the salmon into bite-sized pieces.

Put lemon, orange, and lime juices in a shallow glass pan. Add serrano chiles, 2 tablespoons olive oil, scallops, and salmon. Cover and refrigerate for 2 hours. Turn at least once to be sure all the fish is exposed to the marinade. Marinate 2 more hours. Remove fish and discard the marinade.

In another bowl, combine the cilantro, tomatoes, red onion, orange juice, lime juice, and remaining 1 tablespoon olive oil. Add scallops and salmon and season with salt and pepper. Toss gently to combine.

Refrigerate at least one hour before serving.

Add avocado when ready to serve. Divide the ceviche between margarita glasses and garnish with a sprig of fresh cilantro.

NUTRITIONAL ANALYSIS (PER SERVING)
Calories 200 (40% from fat); Protein 23 grams;
Carbohydrates 6 grams; Fiber less than 1 gram; Fat 9 grams.

SHRIMP AND SCALLOP CEVICHE

SERVES 8

Ceviche is usually made from raw fish that is cooked by enzymes in lime juice. In this method, the shellfish are poached before being marinated. You may use any combination of fish and shellfish; however, the fish must be fresh, not frozen. This makes a very light, refreshing appetizer.

Bring water and wine to a rolling boil in a medium-sized saucepan. Add shrimp, scallops, peppercorns, and onion. After 1 minute, remove from heat, cover, and let stand 5 minutes. Strain and cool.

When completely cool, place the shellfish in a shallow container and add the lime juice. Cover and refrigerate 2 to 3 hours.

In a blender or food processor fitted with the metal blade, combine the garlic, cilantro, and serrano chiles and blend well. Add the oil and blend to combine. Add the blended cilantro mixture to the shellfish and mix in well. Season to taste with salt and pepper.

When ready to serve, pour off most of the lime juice mixture and reserve to toss with the thinly sliced spinach leaves and jicama. Add fresh tomatoes to the ceviche and toss to mix.

Place spinach and jicama in a small bowl and toss with reserved lime juice mixture. Place on small appetizer plates. Divide ceviche between the plates and garnish with fresh cilantro sprigs.

3 cups water

2 cups white wine

1 pound fresh shrimp (51–60 count), peeled, tails removed, and cut in half

½ pound fresh bay scallops, halved

1 onion, sliced

peppercorns

1½ cups fresh lime juice

2 garlic cloves, minced

1 cup loosely packed fresh cilantro, stemmed

2 serrano chiles, stemmed and seeded

2 tablespoons safflower oil

½ teaspoon salt

⅛ teaspoon white pepper

1 cup diced fresh tomatoes

2 cups packed thinly sliced baby spinach

½ jicama, thinly sliced and cut into short strips

Garnish
fresh cilantro sprigs

NUTRITIONAL ANALYSIS (PER SERVING)
Calories 148 (33% from fat); Protein 17 grams;
Carbohydrates 7 grams; Fiber 1 gram; Fat 5.5 grams.

1½ pounds cooked frozen salad shrimp, peeled

3 cups Bloody Mary mix

3 tablespoons juice from pickled jalapeños

2 tablespoons fresh lime juice

¾ cup tomato catsup

3 tablespoons picante sauce

1 cup diced seedless cucumber

½ cup diced red onion

Garnishes

1 small avocado, cut into chunks

8 tortilla chips

LOS CABOS SHRIMP COCKTAIL
SERVES 8

Similar to the Mexican version of shrimp ceviche, this dish is made with cooked shrimp. It makes a very appealing first course when served in a martini glass. Since salad shrimp are used, it is also very cost effective. When in season, you can use equal amounts of lobster pieces and shrimp . . . more expensive, but a bit fancier. If you can find catsup without sugar, you will save a few carbs and calories.

You can make the mix several days ahead, but thaw the shrimp the day you plan to serve the cocktail.

If the shrimp is frozen, thaw quickly by placing in a large colander under cold running water and tossing several times to expose all the shrimp to the water. Let drain for about 5 to 8 minutes. This is very important. Thawing shrimp in the refrigerator makes them "fishy."

Combine the Bloody Mary mix with jalapeño juice, lime juice, catsup, picante sauce, cucumber, and onion and mix well. Add drained shrimp. Refrigerate until ready to serve.

Divide the shrimp between 8 martini glasses. Put a few pieces of avocado atop each one, with a tortilla chip in the middle.

**NUTRITIONAL ANALYSIS
(PER SERVING, WITH GARNISH)**
Calories 167 (32% from fat); Protein 21 grams;
Carbohydrates 8 grams; Fiber 1 gram; Fat 6 grams.

QUESADILLAS

Southwesterners have quickly abandoned the traditional Mexican method of preparing quesadillas. I suspect we like our fat hidden. In the old method, corn tortillas were filled with cheese and fried in oil, resulting in a tasty but greasy quesadilla. Today, most quesadillas are prepared with flour tortillas and may be "stacked" or folded before they are toasted on a hot griddle or in a nonstick frying pan. To be sure the fillings are hot, bake them in a preheated oven for 5 to 10 minutes after browning.

Quesadillas may be as simple as melted cheese, onions, and green chiles or try one of the combinations that follow. The procedure for Roasted Pepper and Onion Quesadillas (p. 57) is the same as for Crab Quesadillas (p. 56). Restaurant chefs give free rein to their imaginations, so don't be surprised to find everything from smoked duck to wild mushroom quesadillas on popular menus.

Quesadillas may be prepared 6 to 8 hours in advance. Wrap them in plastic wrap and refrigerate until you are ready to cook.

1 pound lump crabmeat

1 cup chopped onion

⅓ cup each, diced red and green bell peppers

3 tablespoons diced pickled jalapeño chiles

2 ounces light or low-fat cream cheese

2 tablespoons light mayonnaise

2 teaspoons fresh lemon juice

1 tablespoon fresh minced parsley

salt and pepper to taste

10 flour tortillas

1 cup fresh diced tomatoes

5 ounces low-fat Monterey jack cheese or 5 slices non-fat Swiss cheese

Garnishes

Chile Poblano Cream (p. 40)

Grilled Tomato Salsa (p. 30)

CRAB QUESADILLAS

30 WEDGES AS AN APPETIZER

The fresh lump crabmeat from the Texas coast is delicious with spicy chiles. Serve these with your favorite picante sauce and the Chile Poblano Cream. One of my testers prepared these using an imitation crab product and was very pleased with the results. Many wholesale superstores carry some excellent crab products.

Pick over the crabmeat, removing any small bones or cartilage.

Coat a nonstick skillet with vegetable-oil cooking spray and place over medium heat. Sauté onion and bell pepper 1 to 2 minutes to soften. Add jalapeño chiles and cream cheese. Remove from heat and stir the cheese to mix in the cream cheese. In a small bowl, mix the mayonnaise, lemon juice, and parsley. Gently stir in the crabmeat and season to taste with salt and pepper.

Soften flour tortillas 2 or 3 at a time. Spread the crabmeat mixture in the center of a tortilla and fold over. Press down firmly. Open again and top one half of the tortilla with about 1½ tablespoons diced tomatoes and about ½ ounce cheese. Fold and set aside. Prepare remaining tortillas.

When ready to cook the quesadillas, preheat the oven to 350°. Place a nonstick skillet over medium heat and cook quesadillas until lightly browned on both sides. Reduce the heat if they brown too rapidly. Transfer to a cookie sheet and finish baking in the oven 4 to 5 minutes. Cut into 30 wedges and serve with Chile Poblano Cream, Grilled Tomato Salsa, or one of the many fruit salsas.

**NUTRITIONAL ANALYSIS
(PER WEDGE, WITHOUT GARNISH)**

Calories 92 (29% from fat); Protein 6 grams;
Carbohydrates 10 grams; Fiber less than 1 gram; Fat 3 grams.

ROASTED PEPPER AND ONION QUESADILLAS

30 WEDGES AS AN APPETIZER

While brie cheese is high in fat, very little is needed per portion. The flavor and melting texture is hard to replace.

1 onion, halved and cut into thin strips

salt and pepper

1 papaya, peeled and diced

2 poblano chiles, roasted, peeled, and diced

10 flour tortillas

10 ounces brie cheese

Coat a medium skillet with a vegetable-oil cooking spray and place over medium heat. Add onion and sauté until softened and lightly browned, about 2 to 3 minutes. Season with salt and pepper and set aside.

Combine papaya and poblano chiles. Soften the tortillas 2 to 3 at a time. Assemble in the following manner: On half the tortilla, put one-tenth the onion mixture, one-tenth the papaya-chile mixture, and the brie cheese. Cut the brie into very thin slices and place on top. Use about one ounce cheese per tortilla. Fold over and press down firmly. Repeat with remaining tortillas.

Cook tortillas according to the method described in Crab Quesadillas.

NUTRITIONAL ANALYSIS (PER WEDGE)

Calories 93 (39% from fat); Protein 3 grams;
Carbohydrates 11 grams; Fiber less than 1 gram; Fat 4 grams.

---

2 cloves garlic, minced

8 mushrooms, thinly sliced

½ cup diced yellow onion, divided use

salt and pepper

½ cup diced green chiles

⅓ cup diced sun-dried tomatoes

1 10-ounce package frozen spinach, thawed and well drained

3 ounces light or low-fat cream cheese, at room temperature

½–1 teaspoon salt (to taste)

⅛ teaspoon cayenne pepper

1 tablespoon grated Parmesan cheese

8 flour tortillas, 5–6 inches in diameter

½ cup chunky-style picante sauce

6 ounces low-fat Monterey jack or cheddar cheese, grated

Garnish
Pico de Gallo (p. 28)

SPINACH AND MUSHROOM QUESADILLAS

20 WEDGES

Quesadillas are great for snacks or appetizers. Any low-fat or non-fat cheese may be used or omit the cheese completely. In this version the quesadillas are stacked rather than folded.

Preheat the oven to 300°.

Coat a medium nonstick skillet with a vegetable-oil cooking spray. Over medium heat sauté the garlic, mushrooms, and the onion. Turn often, cooking quickly. Season with salt and pepper and set aside. Rinse the pan, and using the same method, sauté the onion, bell pepper, and chiles. Stir in the sun-dried tomatoes, spinach, cream cheese, salt, cayenne pepper, and Parmesan cheese.

To assemble the tortillas, divide the spinach mixture evenly on 4 tortillas. Spread to within ½ inch of the edge. Top with the mushroom mixture, picante sauce, and grated cheese. Put the remaining 4 tortillas on top and press down firmly.

Coat a clean skillet with a vegetable-oil cooking spray and place over medium heat. Cook quesadillas briefly on both sides to brown, then transfer to a cookie sheet and place in the oven to keep warm while cooking the remaining tortillas.

Cut quesadillas in quarters or 30 wedges for serving.

Garnish with Pico de Gallo.

**NUTRITIONAL ANALYSIS
(PER WEDGE, BASED ON 20 WEDGES
PER RECIPE, WITHOUT GARNISH)**
Calories 108 (33% from fat); Protein 6 grams;
Carbohydrates 13 grams; Fiber 1 gram; Fat 4 grams.

TORTILLA PIZZAS

Often called "tostaditos," these mini snacks are like a little chalupa. You may use flour or corn tortillas as a base or miniature phyllo cups found in the freezer section of the supermarket. Some fillings can be served in endive leaves, cutting carbs even further. Hot or cold, these make colorful appetizers at a cocktail party. Many specialty supermarkets have an array of pre-made salsa and pestos, making these delightful appetizers a breeze.

corn or flour 6-inch tortillas or 3-inch pita rounds, halved

butter-flavored cooking spray

salt

TORTILLAS

Preheat the oven to 350°.

Cut tortillas into 3-inch rounds. Coat both sides of the tortillas with a butter-flavored cooking spray and sprinkle lightly with salt. Bake on a cookie sheet for 8 minutes or until crisp. Toast halved pita rounds in the same way.

SHRIMP AND GUACAMOLE PIZZA

Spread the guacamole on the toasted tortilla. Season the shrimp with salt and pepper and place on top. Garnish with picante sauce or Mango Salsa.

1 tablespoon Skinny Guacamole (p. 44)

1 cooked shrimp

salt and pepper

Garnish

picante sauce or Mango Salsa (p. 35)

**NUTRITIONAL ANALYSIS
(PER TORTILLA, WITHOUT GARNISH)**

Calories 59 (% from fat); Protein 3 grams;
Carbohydrates 7 grams; Fiber 1 gram; Fat 2.5 grams.

BLACK BEAN & MANGO PIZZA

Spread the tortilla with Mashed Black Beans. Top with Mango Salsa.

Mashed Black Beans (p. 18)

Mango Salsa (p. 35)

1 tablespoon light sour cream

shredded romaine lettuce

NUTRITIONAL ANALYSIS (PER TORTILLA)

Calories 83 (16% from fat); Protein 6 grams;
Carbohydrates 13 grams; Fiber 1 gram; Fat 4 grams.

---

2 tablespoons shredded,
seasoned chicken

1 tablespoon grated Havarti
or pepperjack cheese

1 tablespoon Pico de Gallo
(p. 28)

CHICKEN AND CHEESE PIZZA

Preheat oven to 400°. Place toasted tortilla rounds on a cookie sheet. Top with shredded chicken and grated cheese. Bake 5 to 8 minutes or until the cheese is melted. Top with Pico de Gallo.

> **NUTRITIONAL ANALYSIS (PER TORTILLA)**
> Calories 87 (36% from fat); Protein 7 grams;
> Carbohydrates 7 grams; Fiber 1 gram; Fat 3.5 grams.

2 tablespoons Taco Meat
(p. 140)

shredded lettuce

¼ ounce crumbled cotija
cheese

diced jalapeño chiles

TACO PIZZA

Heat the Taco Meat in a small skillet. Spoon on toasted tortillas. Top with sour cream, lettuce, cotija cheese, and jalapeño chiles.

> **NUTRITIONAL ANALYSIS (PER TORTILLA)**
> Calories 95 (43% from fat); Protein 7 grams;
> Carbohydrates 7 grams; Fiber 1 gram; Fat 4.5 grams.

½ ounce grilled diced
chicken, seasoned
chicken broth

salt and pepper

1 tablespoon Chile Poblano
Cream (p. 40)

1 slice Roma tomato

CHICKEN POBLANO PIZZA

Heat the grilled chicken in a small skillet coated with a vegetable-oil cooking spray. Add a little chicken broth to moisten. Season with salt and pepper. Put chicken on the tortilla and top with Chile Poblano Cream and a tomato slice.

> **NUTRITIONAL ANALYSIS (PER TORTILLA)**
> Calories 107 (46% from fat); Protein 7 grams;
> Carbohydrates 8 grams; Fiber 1 gram; Fat 5.5 grams.

TOSTADA GRANDE

SERVES 16

low-fat, low-carb

This recipe will remind you of a giant quesadilla or stacked enchilada. Cut it into wedges or squares and serve it on a pizza stone for a Southwest buffet.

Preheat the oven to 350°.

Place flour tortillas directly on the rack and bake 4 minutes to toast. Tortillas will not be crisp.

Coat a pizza pan or pizza stone with a vegetable-oil cooking spray. Put one tortilla on the pan and top with mashed beans and chicken. Sprinkle with salt, pepper, and chili powder. Top with the second tortilla.

Combine the cream cheese, ricotta, and Romano cheese in a food processor fitted with the metal blade. Season with salt and pepper and spread on top of the second tortilla.

Place a small skillet over medium heat and sauté the chiles and onion in butter until softened, about 2 minutes. Put on top of the cheese mixture. Put the third tortilla on top of the chiles. Press down firmly.

Bake for 10 minutes, then top with grated cheese and bake 5 to 10 minutes.

Top with the lettuce, tomatoes, and crumbled feta cheese.

3 burrito-sized flour tortillas

1 cup Mashed Black Beans (p. 18)

1½ cups shredded smoked or barbecued chicken

salt and pepper

¼ teaspoon chili powder

2 ounces light or low-fat cream cheese

½ cup low-fat ricotta cheese

2 tablespoons Romano cheese

1 4½-ounce can diced green chiles

1 cup diced onion

1 tablespoon light butter

2 ounces low-fat cheddar cheese, grated

1½ cups thinly sliced romaine or red tip leaf lettuce

1½ cups diced tomatoes

3 ounces feta cheese, crumbled

NUTRITIONAL ANALYSIS (PER SERVING)

Calories 138 (36% from fat); Protein 9 grams;
Carbohydrates 13 grams; Fiber 2 grams; Fat 5.5 grams.

---

1 cup prepared pimiento cheese

⅓ cup grated smoked Gouda cheese

4 diced pickled jalapeño chiles

2 12-inch flour tortillas

⅔ cup thinly sliced leaf lettuce

1 egg white, beaten

PIMIENTO CHEESE ROLL UPS

MAKES 24 SLICES

A quick appetizer, this dish takes about 15 minutes. Make these up to 8 hours in advance.

In a small bowl combine the pimiento cheese, Gouda cheese, and jalapeño chiles.

Warm the tortillas, one at a time, in a microwave oven, on high, for 15 seconds or until soft. Spread the tortilla with half the cheese mixture, leaving a 1-inch border on one side. Sprinkle with lettuce. Roll up tightly, brushing the one inch border with egg white. Press ends together to seal. Wrap the tortilla roll in plastic wrap and repeat with the remaining tortillas. Refrigerate until ready to serve.

Slice the tortillas in 10 to 12 slices, discarding ends. Serve on a platter with picante sauce.

NUTRITIONAL ANALYSIS (PER SLICE)
Calories 54 (33% from fat); Protein 3 grams;
Carbohydrates 6 grams; Fiber less than 1 gram; Fat 2 grams.

SMOKED TURKEY ROLL UPS

MAKES 16 APPETIZERS OR 3 SANDWICHES

These roll ups can be served as an appetizer when sliced thin or, if sliced in thirds, a sandwich. Low-fat flour tortillas have become a popular "low-carb" wrap at many fast-food restaurants. When using well-seasoned, light or low-fat cream cheese, these can be quite low in calories.

4 ounces light or low-fat cream cheese

1 teaspoon adobo sauce from canned chipotle chiles

1 teaspoon dry ranch dressing seasoning mix

a few sprigs fresh basil (optional)

2 12-inch flour tortillas

4–5 leaves of red tip or leaf lettuce

16 thin smoked turkey slices

2 ounces smoked Gouda cheese, grated

1 tomato, thinly sliced

1 egg white, beaten

Using a food processor fitted with the metal blade, process cream cheese, adobo sauce, ranch dressing seasoning mix, and basil, if using, until smooth. Set aside.

One at a time, microwave flour tortillas on high for 15 seconds to soften. Spread with cream cheese mixture. Leave one edge with a 1-inch border in order to seal the roll ups.

Arrange one layer of lettuce over the cream cheese, half the turkey slices, half the grated cheese, and half the tomato slices. Tightly roll up the tortilla, brushing the 1-inch border with egg white. Press to seal. Place seam side down on plastic wrap and seal. Repeat with the second tortilla. Refrigerate until ready to serve.

APPETIZERS

Cut each tortilla into 8 thin slices, discarding the ends.

SANDWICHES

Cut each tortilla on the diagonal into 3 portions. Serve 2 per person along with a cup of soup or small salad.

NUTRITIONAL ANALYSIS (PER APPETIZER)

Calories 81 (33% from fat); Protein 5 grams;
Carbohydrates 8 grams; Fiber less than 1 gram; Fat 3 grams.

Salsa

1 red bell pepper, roasted,
    peeled, and diced

2 Roma tomatoes, diced

3 tablespoons diced red
    onion, rinsed

1 tablespoon minced fresh
    basil

1 tablespoon minced fresh
    cilantro

2 ounces anejo cheese,
    crumbled

1 tablespoon olive oil

salt and pepper

Fish

juice from ½ lemon

8 ounces fresh swordfish

olive oil

salt and pepper

endive cups, toasted phyllo
    shells, or toasted French
    bread

Cilantro Cream (p. 22)

SWORDFISH BOATS WITH ROASTED PEPPERS

MAKES 3 CUPS OR 28 APPETIZERS

This "salsa" can be served in endive cups, toasted phyllo shells, or on toasted French bread like a bruschetta. Nutritional information is for the filling only.

To make the salsa, combine the bell pepper, tomatoes, onion, basil, cilantro, cheese, and olive oil in a small glass bowl and season to taste with salt and pepper.

Prepare a grill on high heat. Squeeze lemon juice over the fish and let stand 10 minutes. Brush the fish generously with olive oil and season with salt and pepper. Grill covered about 8 minutes per inch of thickness. If you bake the fish in a 375° oven, increase the time to 12 to 15 minutes per inch of thickness. Place fish on a large plate, cool a few minutes, them cut into small pieces. Add fish to the salsa and toss gently to keep the swordfish from breaking up. Spoon into endive cups, toasted phyllo shells, or toasted French bread. Put the Cilantro Cream in a squirt bottle and drizzle some over each appetizer. Serve immediately.

NUTRITIONAL ANALYSIS (PER APPETIZER)

Calories 27 (50% from fat); Protein 2 grams;
Carbohydrates less than 1 gram; Fiber less than 1 gram;
Fat 1.5 grams.

SMOKED SALMON TORTILLA BITES

MAKES 24

These are surprisingly low in fat and carbohydrates and make a colorful "do ahead" appetizer.

Advance preparation: Rolls may be prepared up to 12 hours in advance.

Using a food processor fitted with the metal blade, process cream cheese and cucumber to combine. Set aside.

Doing one tortilla at a time, place tortilla on paper towel and microwave 10 to 15 seconds to soften.

Spread the tortilla with half the cream cheese mixture, leaving a ½-inch border on 3 sides, and a 1½-inch border on one side. Sprinkle with half the peppers and half the onion. Top with half the salmon and half the spinach strips. Brush the 1½-inch border with egg white.

Starting with the opposite edge, tightly roll up the tortilla, pressing edges together.

Lay seam side down on plastic wrap. Repeat with remaining tortilla and enclose both tortillas in plastic wrap. Refrigerate until ready to slice and serve.

Using a sharp knife, cut away ends of tortilla roll and discard. Cut the tortilla into 12 round slices.

Serve on a tray garnished with fresh parsley, or serve with the Cilantro Cream dipping sauce.

NUTRITIONAL ANALYSIS (PER BITE, WITHOUT GARNISH)
Calories 57 (39% from fat); Protein 3 grams;
Carbohydrates 5 grams; Fiber less than 1 gram; Fat 2.5 grams.

---

low-fat, low-carb

8 ounces light or low-fat cream cheese

⅓ cup diced seedless cucumber

2 12-inch burrito-sized tortillas, preferably spinach flavored

⅓ cup diced red bell pepper

⅓ cup diced yellow bell pepper

⅓ cup diced red onion

6 ounces sliced smoked salmon

1 cup fresh spinach, cut into thin strips

1 egg white, beaten

Garnishes

parsley sprigs

Cilantro Cream (p. 22)

1 clove garlic

1 scallion, both green and
white parts

1 ounce cheddar or
American cheese, grated

5 ounces light or low-fat
cream cheese

2 tablespoons diced
pimiento

1 tablespoon light
mayonnaise

3–4 sprigs fresh parsley

⅛ teaspoon cayenne pepper

¼ teaspoon salt

4 ounces fresh lump
crabmeat

2 12-inch burrito-sized flour
tortillas

1 cup baby spinach or
arugula leaves

1 egg white, beaten

SPICY CRAB
TORTILLA BITES

MAKES 24–26 PIECES

Prepare these appetizers using the same method as the Smoked Salmon Tortilla Bites, only in a different order. Serve them with the Quick Winter Salsa (p. 32) or your favorite picante sauce. Fresh lump crabmeat is always the best, but when out of season, try using frozen Alaskan king crab.

Advance Preparation: Rolls may be made 12 hours in advance.

Using a food processor fitted with the metal blade, process garlic, scallion, cheddar or American cheese, and cream cheese until smooth. Add pimiento, mayonnaise, parsley, cayenne pepper, and salt and process briefly to combine. Using the on/off switch, pulse in the crabmeat.

Microwave one tortilla at a time on high for 15 seconds to soften. Spread tortillas first with half the crab mixture, then arrange a row of half the spinach or arugula on top. (See Smoked Salmon Bites, p. 65, and use the method shown.)

Brush the exposed edge with egg white, then roll up and seal. Repeat with the remaining tortilla and wrap both in plastic wrap until ready to cut into pieces.

When ready to serve, cut away the ends of the tortillas and discard. Cut tortilla rolls into 12 pieces and arrange on a serving platter. Garnish with fresh sprigs of parsley and serve with your favorite salsa or picante sauce.

**NUTRITIONAL ANALYSIS (PER BITE,
BASED ON 24 BITES PER RECIPE)**
Calories 50 (36% from fat); Protein 3 grams;
Carbohydrates 5 grams; Fiber less than 1 gram; Fat 2 grams.

CHILE CHEESE PUFFS

MAKES 36 PHYLLO CUPS OR 9 SQUARES

This versatile recipe can be an appetizer, first course, or a light luncheon dish. The poblano chiles give a distinctive flavor that is very different from canned or frozen green chiles. A food processor is necessary to purée the cottage cheese.

These may also be prepared in miniature muffin tins, yielding about 36. Chile Cheese Puffs make good appetizers to pass and can be made ahead and reheated. See the note at the end of the recipe for this variation.

6 large eggs

1 cup low-fat cottage cheese

1 cup grated Havarti cheese

1 cup grated reduced-fat Monterey jack cheese

½ cup diced onion

2 poblano chiles, roasted, peeled, and coarsely chopped

2 teaspoons baking powder

1 teaspoon salt

pinch cayenne pepper

¼ cup all-purpose flour

36 phyllo cups (optional)

Preheat oven to 350°.

Using a food processor fitted with the metal blade, process eggs, cottage cheese, and grated cheeses until well combined, about 1 minute. Add onion, chiles, baking powder, salt, and cayenne pepper. Pulse with on/off switch to combine. Add flour and pulse a few times to combine.

Prepare the Chile Cheese Puffs according to one of the following:

Phyllo Cups: Arrange phyllo cups on a baking sheet. Spoon the mixture into phyllo cups, about ⅞ full. Bake 15 minutes or until soft set. Serve with a dollop of salsa on top.

Baking Dish: Coat an 8 × 8 × 2 baking dish with a vegetable-oil cooking spray. Pour into the prepared baking pan. Bake 30 minutes or until puffed, lightly browned, and soft set. Cut into 9 squares and serve with salsa. If this is a luncheon dish, serve with Simple Mixed Green Salad with Toasted Pecan Vinaigrette (p. 87).

NUTRITIONAL ANALYSIS (PER SQUARE, BASED ON 9 SQUARES PER RECIPE)

Calories 185 (49% from fat); Protein 17 grams; Carbohydrates 6 grams; Fiber less than 1 gram; Fat 10 grams.

Note: For an appetizer to pass, you can bake this in miniature muffin tins. In this case, prepare the muffin tins with a vegetable-oil cooking spray. Fill about ¾ full. Bake 15 minutes or until soft set. Serve topped with a dollop of salsa. Makes 36.

4

Salads

In the past, Southwest restaurants have used lettuces to garnish combination plates, and salads have been limited to Taco Salads, which can weigh in heavy on fat and calories—some in excess of 900 calories and 60 fat grams. Today, even Mexican restaurants have expanded their salad selections to include Caesar Salads and salads made with fajita chicken and shrimp.

Southwest cuisine has embraced many new salads using a variety of greens, fruits, and vegetables to create salads that can be appetizers as well as entrées.

Studies have shown that many people consume more fat grams and calories from salad dressings, mayonnaise, and cheese than any other food, so there are some significant savings to be found here. Vinaigrettes are lightened, cheese is limited or low-fat, and flavors and textures are emphasized by using fruits, vegetables, and oven-fried tortilla strips. You'll find light versions of your favorite beef and chicken Taco Salad (p. 79), Caesar Salad (p. 72), Smoked Turkey Salad (p. 81), Tequila-Orange Salad (p. 69), and a colorful, spicy Southwest Bean Salad (p. 76).

TEQUILA-ORANGE SALAD

SERVES 6

This is a very light refreshing salad that pairs nicely with spicy foods. If you are limiting carbs, use the toasted almonds in place of the tortillas and omit the orange sections.

Most packaged greens have been pre-washed. Simply sort through them, discarding any wilted pieces. Lightly mist with water, dry thoroughly and store in paper towel-lined plastic bags to re-crisp.

To section the oranges, cut off both ends and discard. Use a sharp knife to cut away the peel and membrane. Cut between sections to remove perfect wedges. Squeeze the juice from remaining pulp and reserve.

Toss the greens with orange sections, bell pepper or sun-dried tomatoes, jicama, and just enough Tequila-Orange Vinaigrette (p. 70) to lightly coat the greens. Toss again with tortilla strips or toasted almonds and divide among 6 salad plates.

Salad

2 5-ounce packages "spring mix" greens

4 seedless oranges, sectioned, juice reserved

1 red bell pepper, cut into thin, short strips or ½ cup sun-dried tomatoes

1½ cups thinly sliced (and cut into short strips) jicama

4 toasted Tortilla Strips, 4 tortillas (p. 9) or ⅓ cup sliced almonds, toasted

---

**NUTRITIONAL ANALYSIS
(PER SERVING, SALAD,
WITHOUT DRESSING)**

Calories 185 (24% from fat); Protein 7 grams;
Carbohydrates 28 grams; Fiber 6 grams; Fat 5 grams.

Vinaigrette

1 large shallot, minced

1 small knob fresh ginger, grated

1 ounce tequila

¼ cup reserved orange juice

1½ ounces Triple Sec or any orange liqueur

1 small clove garlic

1½ teaspoons Dijon mustard

a few drops of chili oil

4 tablespoons rice wine vinegar

½–⅔ cup safflower oil

1 teaspoon soy sauce

a few sprigs of fresh parsley

salt

Note: This vinaigrette can replace a sauce on grilled fish such as mahimahi, salmon, or swordfish. You can serve the grilled fish on a bed of wild rice with fresh asparagus, topped with the vinaigrette. The result is a very low-fat, low-calorie, low-carb entrée.

TEQUILA-ORANGE VINAIGRETTE

Put the shallot, ginger, tequila, reserved orange juice, and Triple Sec in a small saucepan and bring to a boil. Boil 3 to 4 minutes or until reduced by about ⅓ the volume. Put garlic, mustard, and reduced orange mixture in a blender jar. Add chili oil and vinegar and blend until smooth. With the blender running, slowly add the safflower oil through the top, blending until smooth and emulsified. Add soy sauce and parsley and blend again. Season to taste with salt.

**NUTRITIONAL ANALYSIS
(PER TABLESPOON,
BASED ON 1½ CUPS PER RECIPE,
USING ONLY ½-CUP SAFFLOWER OIL)**

Calories 59 (83% from fat); Protein less than 1 gram;
Carbohydrates less than 1 gram; Fiber less than 1 gram;
Fat 5.5 grams.

SPINACH CORN SALAD

SERVES 5–6

This is another light salad that is delicious with the Tequila-Orange Vinaigrette. You can use jicama in place of the red bell peppers or a mixture of baby lettuces in place of the spinach.

Cut the spinach or arugula into bite-sized pieces and toss with the roasted peppers, corn, cheese, and asparagus tips. Add enough vinaigrette to moisten.

Divide the salad between 5 or 6 serving plates. Serve each one with cracked black pepper, lime wedges, and tortilla strips.

NUTRITIONAL ANALYSIS (PER SERVING, BASED ON 6 SERVINGS PER RECIPE WITH 1½ TABLESPOONS VINAIGRETTE)

Calories 191 (52% from fat); Protein 10 grams; Carbohydrates 14 grams; Fiber 3 grams; Fat 13 grams.

---

1 pound fresh baby spinach or arugula, rinsed

2 red bell peppers, roasted, peeled, and cut into short strips

1½ cups fresh white corn kernels, cut from the cob and blanched 1 minute

3 ounces anejo or Parmesan cheese, shaved

12 asparagus tips, blanched 1 minute

Tequila-Orange Vinaigrette (p. 70)

freshly cracked black pepper

lime wedges

tortilla strips

Salad

1 large head romaine lettuce

1 cup fresh corn kernels

1 cup diced tomatoes, preferably Roma

2 ounces grated Parmesan or romano cheese

25 purchased croutons

Dressing

1 garlic clove

½ teaspoon anchovy paste

1 tablespoon Worcestershire sauce

2 teaspoons Dijon mustard

juice from 1 lemon

2 tablespoons balsamic or sherry vinegar

2 tablespoons grated Romano cheese

½ teaspoon salt

pinch white pepper

4 tablespoons safflower oil

1 egg white

Optional

1 pound fresh shrimp, cooked

4 skinless boneless chicken breast halves, grilled and cut into bite-sized pieces

CAESAR SALAD

SERVES 5

Traditional Caesar salads can be laden with hidden fat. In this version, fat and calories have been trimmed by more than half. Try the shrimp and chicken variations at the end of the recipe, and you can make one of the most popular restaurant salads at home, with half the fat and calories. There are many varieties of prepared croutons available. Choose those with a low-carb and calorie count and allow 4 to 5 per salad.

Rinse and dry the lettuce thoroughly. Cut leaves down the center rib and chop into bite-sized pieces. Store the lettuce in resealable bags lined with paper towels.

To prepare the dressing, put the garlic, anchovy paste, mustard, and lemon juice in a blender jar or food processor fitted with the metal blade and blend smooth. Add the cheese, salt, and pepper. While the blender runs, pour the oil and egg white through the top. Set aside.

When you are ready to serve the salad, drop the corn kernels into boiling salted water for 1 minute to blanch. Or microwave for 40 seconds on high. Refresh under cold water. Toss the chilled lettuce with corn, tomatoes, cheese, and just enough Caesar Dressing to lightly coat the greens.

Crush 5 croutons per salad and put atop the greens.

Divide the salad between 5 salad plates and garnish with cheese.

NUTRITIONAL ANALYSIS (PER SERVING, SALAD ONLY, WITHOUT SHRIMP OR CHICKEN, WITH 1½ TABLESPOONS DRESSING)
Calories 191 (52% from fat); Protein 6 grams; Carbohydrates 13 grams; Fiber 1 gram; Fat 11 grams.

NUTRITIONAL ANALYSIS (PER SERVING, SALAD WITH SHRIMP, WITHOUT DRESSING)
Calories 201 (25% from fat); Protein 25 grams; Carbohydrates 12 grams; Fiber ; Fat 5.5 grams.

NUTRITIONAL ANALYSIS (PER SERVING, SALAD WITH CHICKEN, WITHOUT DRESSING)
Calories 326 (25% from fat); Protein 48 grams; Carbohydrates 12 grams; Fiber 1 gram; Fat 9.5 grams.

CAESAR DRESSING

Put the garlic, anchovy paste, Worcestershire sauce, mustard, and lemon juice in a blender jar or food processor fitted with the metal blade and blend until smooth. Add the vinegar, cheese, salt, and pepper. With the blender running, pour the oil and egg white through the top. Set aside.

**NUTRITIONAL ANALYSIS
(PER TABLESPOON,
BASED ON ¾-CUP PER RECIPE)**

Calories 53 (85% from fat); Protein less than 1 gram;
Carbohydrates 1 gram; Fiber less than 1 gram; Fat 5 grams.

Shrimp or Chicken Variations: If preparing a Shrimp or Chicken Caesar, cook the shrimp or chicken ahead. Toss with the greens and place 4 to 5 pieces on top after tossing the salad.

½ cup bottled, refrigerated Caesar dressing

¼ cup water

¼ teaspoon anchovy paste

½ teaspoon Dijon mustard

2 dashes Worcestershire sauce

3 heads hearts of romaine lettuce

¾ cup canned onion rings

18–20 cherry tomatoes, halved

½ cup grated anejo cheese or string Parmesan cheese

QUICK LOW-CARB CAESAR

SERVES 6

The carbs in a Caesar Salad come mainly from the croutons (though even these are fairly low) and the fat from the dressing. This method lowers fat, carbs, and calories. The onion rings replace croutons, adding very few carbs but a nice flavor.

Preheat oven to 350°.

To make the dressing, whisk together prepared Caesar dressing with water, anchovy paste, mustard, and Worcestershire sauce. Refrigerate at least an hour.

Rinse romaine hearts under cold water and dry thoroughly. Cut into bite-sized pieces, dry on paper towels in refrigerator and then store in resealable bags lined with paper towels to chill until ready to use.

Put onion rings on a cookie sheet and bake 4 to 5 minutes to lightly toast.

When ready to serve the salad, toss lettuce with tomatoes, cheese, and about ½ cup of the dressing. Divide among 6 salad plates and top each salad with toasted onion rings.

NUTRITIONAL ANALYSIS (PER SERVING)
Calories 185 (66% from fat): Protein 8 grams;
Carbohydrates 8 grams; Fiber 2 grams; Fat 13.5 grams.

WANDA'S CORN SALAD

SERVES 8

My friend Wanda Wheatly served this salad at a casual dinner party, and it was a tremendous hit with both the men and women. Any healthful recipe that has this much appeal is a winner. Because this salad is best made a day ahead, it is a perfect dish for summer entertaining or to accompany grilled meats, chicken, or fish.

Combine the corn, cucumber, tomatoes, bell peppers, chiles, and red onion in a large bowl. Season with salt, pepper, and celery seed.

Combine the mayonnaise, sour cream, and vinegar in a small mixing bowl. Toss with the vegetables and refrigerate, covered, overnight.

NUTRITIONAL ANALYSIS (PER SERVING)
Calories 203 (13% from fat); Protein 6 grams;
Carbohydrates 38 grams; Fiber 6 grams; Fat 3 grams.

---

3 11-ounce cans white corn

1 large cucumber, peeled, seeded, and diced

2 large tomatoes, chopped

2 small green bell peppers, chopped

1 4½-ounce can diced green chiles

1 small red onion, chopped

2 teaspoons salt

½ teaspoon pepper

½ teaspoon celery seed

3 tablespoons light mayonnaise

2 tablespoons light sour cream

2 tablespoons rice wine vinegar

Salad

1 15-ounce can black beans,
  drained
1 cup cooked pinto or
  garbanzo beans
1 bunch scallions, sliced
  (green and white part)
1½ cups diced jicama
1½ cups fresh corn kernels,
  blanched
1 cup chopped red bell
  pepper
½ cup diced firm papaya or
  mango
salt and pepper

Vinaigrette

3 garlic cloves
5 tablespoons fresh lime or
  lemon juice
1 serrano chili, stemmed
  and seeded (optional)
2 tablespoons vinegar
1 teaspoon Dijon mustard
pinch sugar
½ cup safflower oil
2 sprigs fresh parsley
1 sprig fresh mint
½ teaspoon oregano
½ teaspoon salt

SOUTHWEST BEAN SALAD

SERVES 8

Use whatever vegetables, beans, or combination of beans and vegetables that appeal to you or are fresh and seasonal. Black beans make a substantial base and give the salad wonderful color contrast.

To make the vinaigrette, place the garlic in a blender jar and blend to mince. Add the lime or lemon juice and serrano chile and blend again. Add vinegar, mustard, sugar, oil, parsley, mint, oregano, and salt and blend until smooth.

Combine the beans, scallions, jicama, corn, pepper, and papaya or mango in a bowl. Toss well with vinaigrette and adjust salt and pepper to taste. Refrigerate for 4 to 5 hours before serving.

NUTRITIONAL ANALYSIS (PER SERVING)

Calories 249 (47% from fat); Protein 7 grams;
Carbohydrates 25 grams; Fiber 7 grams; Fat 13 grams.

WINTER GREENS WITH CRANBERRIES AND PECANS

SERVES 8 AS AN APPETIZER
OR 5 TO 6 AS AN ENTRÉE

This salad pairs well with almost anything or could be made into an entrée salad by adding chicken or smoked turkey. I have given two vinaigrette choices since the Raspberry Chipotle sauce is sometimes hard to find. You can buy pre-cooked bacon to make preparation much easier with less clean up.

To make the vinaigrette, combine all the ingredients and mix well. If making the Raspberry Chipotle vinaigrette, combine all the ingredients, then strain to remove the seeds. Adjust salt to taste. Set aside.

Using scissors, trim as much fat as possible from the bacon and cut into small pieces. Place on a paper towel and microwave a few seconds to warm and "crisp."

Toss the greens with just enough vinaigrette to moisten (you will use about half of the recipe), bacon, pecans and cranberries. Divide the salad between salad plates, being sure each plate has all the ingredients as the bacon, pecans and berries tend to fall to the bottom. Top with crumbled cheese of choice.

NUTRITIONAL ANALYSIS (WITH 1½ TABLESPOONS VINAIGRETTE AND 4 OUNCES OF CHEESE, PER APPETIZER SERVING)

Calories 215 (67% from fat); Protein 7 grams; Carbohydrates 10 grams; Fiber 2 grams; Fat 16 grams.

NUTRITIONAL ANALYSIS (WITH 1½ TABLESPOONS RASPBERRY CHIPOTLE VINAIGRETTE AND 4 OUNCES OF CHEESE, PER APPETIZER SERVING)

Calories 181 (57% from fat); Protein 8 grams; Carbohydrates 12 grams; Fiber 2 grams; Fat 11.5 grams.

Vinaigrette

⅓ cup light olive oil

¼ cup red wine or balsamic vinegar

1 package sugar substitute

2 tablespoons spring water

salt and pepper to taste

Raspberry Chipotle Vinaigrette

⅔ cups Raspberry Chipotle sauce

¼ cup spring water

¼ cup light olive oil

¼ cup balsamic vinegar

¼ teaspoon salt

Salad

2 packages Mixed Field Greens

8 slices pre-cooked bacon

½ cup coarsely chopped pecans, toasted

½ sun dried cranberries or craisins

4–6 ounces fat free feta or gorgonzola cheese, crumbled

Note: if serving as an entrée salad, simply toss grilled chicken with the greens, or, mound shaved smoked turkey slices on top, drizzled with a small amount of vinaigrette.

Marinade

1 8-ounce bottle prepared
  Italian dressing

2 tablespoons soy sauce

3 cloves fresh minced garlic

3 serrano chilies, chopped

Salad

5 boneless, skinless chicken
  breasts

½ head iceberg lettuce,
  thinly sliced

½ head romaine lettuce,
  chopped into bite-sized
  pieces

½ head leaf lettuce, chopped
  into bite-sized pieces

1 large onion, thinly sliced

1 red bell pepper, cut into
  julienne strips

1 yellow bell pepper, cut
  into julienne strips

1 green bell pepper, cut into
  julienne strips

3 flour tortillas, toasted

2 ounces low-fat Monterey
  jack cheese, grated

2 ounces low-fat cheddar
  cheese, grated

Dressing

fat-free ranch dressing

picante sauce

GRILLED CHICKEN SALAD
SERVES 5

This entrée salad is best prepared in individual servings rather than
a large bowl. It makes a perfect summer supper or lunch entrée.

Three or four hours in advance, combine the Italian dressing,
soy sauce, garlic, and serrano chiles and marinate the chicken
breasts.

When ready to prepare the salad, heat an outdoor grill to
the highest setting. Remove chicken from the marinade and
season on both sides with salt and pepper. Grill the chicken until well marked and the edges take on a "cooked" appearance,
about 4 to 5 minutes. Turn to grill the opposite side for 3 to
4 minutes, depending on the thickness of the chicken.

Combine the lettuces and divide among 5 dinner plates.

Coat a large skillet with a vegetable-oil cooking spray and
place over medium heat. Add onions and peppers and sauté until lightly browned, tossing frequently. You will have to use additional spray to prevent burning. Put onion and peppers on top
of the greens and toss with lettuces.

Preheat the oven to broil. Put toasted tortillas on a cookie
sheet and sprinkle with both cheeses. Broil on the top rack a few
minutes until cheese melts. Cut the tortillas into 6 wedges and
put around the edges of the plates. Slice the chicken breast diagonally with a sharp knife, cutting each breast into 4 or 5 slices.
Arrange on top of the salads.

Serve the salads with ranch dressing and picante sauce.

**NUTRITIONAL ANALYSIS
(PER SERVING, WITHOUT DRESSING)**

Calories 399 (29% from fat); Protein 56 grams;
Carbohydrates 13 grams; Fiber 2 grams; Fat 13.5 grams.

TACO SALAD

SERVES 4

Serve this popular salad in flour tortilla "bowls" or layer it in a 2-quart bowl and serve on a buffet table. Either way, you will not miss a salad dressing, which can run up the calories and fat grams.

Clean lettuces and cut into bite-sized pieces. Dry thoroughly and place in resealable bags lined with paper towels. Refrigerate to "crisp" lettuces. Drain pinto beans and reserve the liquid. Season the beans with salt and pepper. Sear the onion in a small skillet coated with vegetable-oil cooking spray over medium heat.

Remove onion and stir in 3 to 4 tablespoons of the bean liquid. Toss with the pinto beans.

To assemble the salad in a bowl: Put about half the lettuce in a bowl. Scatter ⅔ of the bean mixture on top, half the tomatoes on top of the beans, then half the Skinny Guacamole and tortilla strips. Sprinkle with cheese. Repeat with a second layer in this order: all the chicken, guacamole, beans, and tortilla strips. Arrange remaining cheese around the edge of the bowl.

To assemble the salad in a tortilla bowl: Prepare the bowl as directed on p. 10. Toss the lettuces with the beans and place them in the tortilla bowl. Arrange chicken, grated cheese, and tomatoes on top. Put guacamole in the center. Place the tortilla bowl on a bed of sliced lettuce and a few tortilla strips.

½ head iceberg lettuce

1 small head romaine lettuce or leaf lettuce

1 16-ounce can pinto beans

salt and pepper

1 cup chopped onion

2 cups diced tomatoes

Skinny Guacamole (p. 44)

3 ounces low-fat cheddar or Monterey jack cheese, grated

2½ cups cooked chicken, well-seasoned, or Taco Meat (p. 140)

8 corn tortillas, cut into strips and toasted

NUTRITIONAL ANALYSIS (PER SERVING WITH CHICKEN)

Calories 543 (31% from fat): Protein 48 grams; Carbohydrates 46 grams; Fiber 16 grams; Fat 18.5 grams.

NUTRITIONAL ANALYSIS (PER SERVING WITH TACO MEAT)

Calories 644 (28% from fat): Protein 41 grams; Carbohydrates 75 grams; Fiber 18 grams; Fat 20 grams.

Salad

1 head red tip leaf lettuce
½ head romaine lettuce
1 cup very thinly sliced red
cabbage or radicchio

6 skinless boneless chicken
breast halves, grilled
salt and pepper
1 red bell pepper, cut into
short strips
1 papaya, peeled and diced
1½ cup diced tomatoes
1 small avocado, diced
8 corn tortillas cut into thin
strips and toasted
¼ cup Chile Poblano Cream
(p. 40)

Vinaigrette

1 clove garlic
2 tablespoons fresh lemon
juice
2 tablespoons fresh lime
juice
1 tablespoon honey
2 tablespoons white wine
vinegar
1 tablespoon Dijon mustard
⅓ cup safflower oil
½ teaspoon salt
¼ teaspoon white pepper
1 egg white
3–4 sprigs parsley

TORTILLA SALAD

SERVES 6

Prepare this salad with shrimp or chicken. The dressing is light, and you need very little because the fresh fruits and tortillas supply a variety of flavor and textures. The Chile Poblano Cream gives just a hint of spice for fun. The fat grams and calories are significantly less without the avocado.

Advance Preparation: The chicken and the dressing may be prepared a day in advance. The avocado and papaya may be cut 3 or 4 hours in advance and refrigerated with the dressing.

Rinse and thoroughly dry the lettuces. Toss together in a large bowl.

Slice grilled chicken in short julienne strips and season with salt and pepper. Toss chicken, bell pepper, papaya, tomatoes, avocado, half the tortilla strips, and lettuces with enough Lemon Garlic Vinaigrette to coat. Divide the salad between six serving plates.

Garnish each plate with the remaining tortilla strips in the center of each salad. Put the Chile Poblano Cream in a resealable bag and snip a corner with scissors. Drizzle on top of each salad.

NUTRITIONAL ANALYSIS (PER SERVING)
Calories 470 (26% from fat); Protein 59 grams;
Carbohydrates 28 grams; Fiber 6 grams; Fat 13.5 grams.

LEMON GARLIC VINAIGRETTE

Put the garlic, lemon juice, and lime juice in the blender and blend to mince the garlic. Add honey, vinegar, and mustard and blend until smooth. With the blender running, add the oil, salt, pepper, egg white, and parsley. Adjust seasonings to taste.

NUTRITIONAL ANALYSIS
(PER TABLESPOON,
BASED ON 1 CUP PER RECIPE)
Calories 48 (84% from fat); Protein less than 1 gram;
Carbohydrates 1 gram; Fiber less than 1 gram; Fat 4.5 grams.

SMOKED TURKEY SALAD

SERVES 6

This is my favorite entrée salad. I have prepared it with a variety of smoked meats, from duck to pheasant. It is very colorful and light and may be served as an entrée luncheon salad for 5 or 6 or an appetizer salad for 8 people. The different flavors, textures, and slightly spicy dressing make an attractive, interesting combination.

To make the dressing, bring the chicken broth or stock, wine, and shallots to a boil in a small saucepan. Boil 3 to 4 minutes or until reduced by about half. Put shallots in a blender jar and add mustard, lemon juice, and serrano chile. Blend until smooth. With the blender running, add the egg white, salt, sugar, and safflower oil. Set aside.

Core lettuce and separate into leaves. Rinse and dry thoroughly. Chill until ready to use. Stem and rinse watercress or arugula.

Toss vegetables, turkey, and dressing together.

Arrange lettuce leaves on six serving plates. Place watercress or arugula on top of the lettuce. Toss half the tortilla strips with the meat and vegetables just before serving. Mound the mixture on top of the greens. Garnish with a few black beans and tortilla strips.

NUTRITIONAL ANALYSIS (PER SERVING, BASED ON 6 SERVINGS PER RECIPE)

Calories 257 (58% from fat); Protein 9 grams; Carbohydrates 18 grams; Fiber 5 grams; Fat 16.5 grams.

Note: A rich stock like the Smoked Turkey Stock on page 14 adds a great deal of flavor to this dish. To make a quick version, use meaty bones from a turkey or chicken and place in about 2 cups of canned chicken broth. Boil for about 30 minutes, then cool the broth with the bones in the broth. Strain the stock and refrigerate. Skim all fat. Use ¼ cup in the dressing.

Dressing

½ cup rich chicken broth or Smoked Turkey Stock (p. 14) (see note)
½ cup white wine
2 shallots, minced
2 teaspoons Dijon mustard
1 tablespoon fresh lemon juice
1 serrano chile, stemmed and seeded
1 egg white
1 teaspoon salt
pinch sugar
4 tablespoons safflower oil

Salad

1 head Boston or bibb lettuce
1 bunch watercress or arugula
1 small jicama (about 4 ounces), cut into short julienne strips
1 red bell pepper, cut into short julienne strips
1 yellow bell pepper, cut into short julienne strips
6 ounces French beans (*haricots verts*)
2 carrots, peeled, blanched, and cut into short julienne strips
1¼–1½ pounds smoked turkey breast meat, cut into short julienne strips

Garnishes

½ cup black beans, well seasoned
2 each, red and yellow corn tortillas, in thin strips, toasted (p. 9)

1 fresh grapefruit

6 tablespoon reserved
grapefruit juice

6 tablespoons refrigerated
ranch dressing

⅛ teaspoon cayenne pepper

1 tablespoon minced
cilantro

3 hearts of romaine lettuce

6 ounces queso fresca or
4 ounces mild blue
cheese, crumbled

⅓ cup chopped BBQ Pecans
(p. 26) or almonds

ROMAINE HEARTS WITH CITRUS CILANTRO DRESSING AND BBQ PECANS

SERVES 6

This is a refreshing salad with just a hint of spice in the dressing. Use a refrigerated ranch dressing for a base as the bottled dressings do not give the same result. You could also use canned grapefruit (without sugar), but fresh juice has a brighter flavor.

To section the grapefruit, first cut away both ends and reserve the juice in a measuring cup. Using a sharp knife, cut away grapefruit skin and white membrane. Slice between the membranes to remove sections, then squeeze all remaining juice from the pulp into the measuring cup.

To make the dressing, whisk together grapefruit juice, ranch dressing, cayenne pepper, and cilantro. Chill at least one hour.

Trim away any damaged leaves from the lettuce hearts. Cut the hearts in half, lengthwise, cutting through the core. Place each half romaine heart on a large salad plate. Sprinkle with cheese and nuts, then drizzle with the dressing.

Garnish each salad with a couple of grapefruit sections.

NUTRITIONAL ANALYSIS (PER SERVING)
Calories 199 (79% from fat); Protein 4 grams;
Carbohydrates 6 grams; Fiber 2 grams; Fat 17.5 grams.

CHIPOTLE
CHICKEN SALAD

SERVES 8 AS A SALAD

This low-carb chicken salad has more flavor than the typical celery and mayonnaise chicken salad. If you can buy smoked chicken breasts, the salad is even better.

➡ Serve as an appetizer, in baked phyllo cups or endive leaves

➡ Serve as a salad on mixed greens and garnish with fresh diced tomatoes.

If you are planning to fill phyllo cups, cut the chicken into very small pieces. This is a bit of work, but the end result is very elegant. If not, put the bite-sized pieces in a medium-sized bowl. Add celery, bell pepper, parsley or cilantro, and Chipotle Ranch Dressing. Season to taste with salt and pepper. When ready to serve the salad, toss again and add chopped pecans.

5 chicken breasts, cooked, skinned, boned, and diced, about 5 cups

6–8 stalks celery, diced, about 1½ cups

⅓ cup diced red bell pepper

tablespoon minced parsley or cilantro

½ cup Chipotle Ranch Dressing (p. 25)

salt and pepper

⅓ cup chopped pecans, toasted

NUTRITIONAL ANALYSIS
Calories 262 (39% from fat); Protein 35 grams;
Carbohydrates 4 grams; Fiber less than 1 gram; Fat 11.5 grams.

Shrimp

1½ pounds cooked, frozen
   shrimp (31–40 count)

2 cups water

1 cup fresh corn kernels,
   preferably white corn

1½ cups diced tomatoes

2 tablespoons fresh minced
   cilantro

½ cup ranch dressing,
   refrigerated or freshly
   made

½ cup picante sauce or
   Quick Winter Salsa
   (p. 30)

Salad Base

10 ounces fresh baby
   spinach or arugula

1½ cups jicama, cut into
   short, thin julienne strips

3 tablespoons light olive oil

1 tablespoon fresh lemon
   juice

¼ teaspoon salt

a few twists of black pepper

Note: You can make this
using Chipotle Ranch
Dressing (p. 25) instead
for a spicier version.

SPICY SHRIMP SALAD

SERVES 6 AS A SALAD,
SERVES 8 AS AN APPETIZER

When served in a martini glass, this can be an elegant appetizer. Serve it on a salad plate for a first course salad. If you start with purchased salsa and refrigerated ranch dressing, this is a quick assembly.

Put the shrimp in a colander. Run cold water over the shrimp, tossing to expose all the shrimp and thaw quickly. Remove tails and drain. Set aside 6 to 8 shrimp for garnish. Refrigerate.

In a small saucepan, bring water to a boil over medium high heat. Add corn and return to a boil. Remove immediately, drain, and cool.

In a medium-sized bowl, combine the shrimp, corn, tomatoes, and cilantro. Stir together the ranch dressing and picante sauce or Quick Winter Salsa. Toss with the shrimp mixture and refrigerate until ready to serve.

If serving in a martini glass, cut spinach or arugula into smaller pieces. For a salad, simply remove stems and leave whole.

Toss greens with jicama, olive oil, lemon juice, and salt. Season with black pepper. Arrange greens in the glasses or on salad plates. Mound shrimp mixture on top. Garnish each serving with reserved shrimp, dipped in picante sauce.

NUTRITIONAL ANALYSIS (PER SERVING, BASED ON 6 SALADS PER RECIPE)
Calories 339 (51% from fat); Protein 26 grams;
Carbohydrates 14 grams; Fiber 5 grams; Fat 19.5 grams.

BARBECUE CHICKEN SALAD

SERVES 4

This colorful salad can be made easier by buying a roasted chicken at your supermarket. You may also make it with leftover smoked turkey or roasted pork tenderloin. The roasted chicken actually yields better tasting results because it is very moist.

Preheat the oven to 350°.

To make the dressing, combine the ranch dressing, barbeque sauce, picante sauce or salsa, vinegar, and cayenne pepper and set aside.

Toss the chicken with BBQ seasoning. If using a roasted chicken, be sure to add the drippings when seasoning the chicken.

Combine the greens, chicken, corn, bell pepper, tomatoes, beans, and scallions in a large bowl. Add the dressing and toss to coat all the ingredients.

Put the onion rings on a cookie sheet and toast about 4 minutes. Just before serving, toss them with the salad and divide among 4 salad plates.

NUTRITIONAL ANALYSIS (PER SERVING)

Calories 474 (22% from fat); Protein 39 grams;
Carbohydrates 21 grams; Fiber 6 grams; Fat 26 grams.

Dressing

½ cup ranch dressing

1 tablespoon barbeque sauce (preferably not the sweet variety)

2 tablespoons picante sauce or homemade salsa

½ tablespoon red wine vinegar

pinch of cayenne pepper

Salad

3 cups diced cooked chicken

½ teaspoon BBQ seasoning mix (available in the spice section)

2 5-ounce packages mixed salad greens

¾ cup cooked corn kernels

½ cup diced red bell pepper

12 cherry tomatoes, halved

⅓ cup cooked black beans

4 scallions, trimmed and sliced

¾ cup canned fried onion rings

⅓ cup ranch dressing (from the refrigerated section of the grocery store)

2 tablespoons cold water

3 heads romaine lettuce

¼ head iceberg lettuce

1 rotisserie chicken or 4 cups diced cooked chicken

8 slices lean or reduced fat bacon, cooked until crisp

3 medium tomatoes, chopped

4 ounces cotija cheese, crumbled

1 avocado, diced

1 tablespoon fresh minced parsley

Accent Dressing

Chipotle Ranch Dressing (p. 25) or Chile Poblano Cream (p. 40)

SOUTHWEST COBB SALAD

SERVES 5

You can use a rotisserie chicken, cooked chicken breasts, or turkey, for this salad. While similar to a California Cobb Salad, the cotija cheese gives Southwest Cobb Salad a different flavor. Serve the salad tossed with ranch dressing, then drizzled with an accent dressing such as Chipotle Ranch Dressing or Chile Poblano Cream.

Cook the bacon in a 350° oven on a foil-lined cookie sheet for easier clean up.

Combine the ranch dressing with water and refrigerate at least 1 hour.

Trim away any brown leaves on the romaine, remove the core, and chop into bite-sized pieces. Chop iceberg lettuce into pieces of the same size. Toss together in a large bowl.

Add chicken, bacon, tomatoes, cheese, avocado, and parsley to the greens. Add the ranch dressing and toss to lightly coat the greens. Divide among salad plates.

Put the accent dressing in a squirt bottle and drizzle over the salad.

NUTRITIONAL ANALYSIS (PER SALAD ONLY, WITHOUT ACCENT DRESSING)
Calories 485 (57% from fat); Protein 41 grams;
Carbohydrates 10 grams; Fiber 4 grams; Fat 31 grams.

SIMPLE MIXED GREEN SALAD WITH TOASTED PECAN VINAIGRETTE

SERVES 6

This simple salad with a memorable dressing can precede a Southwest entrée. The crumbly Mexican cheese is a good match for the dressing. Makes 2 cups dressing.

To serve the salad, put lettuce, tomatoes, pecans, and cheese in a bowl. Add about ½ to ⅔ cup of the Toasted Pecan Vinaigrette and toss to coat.

The vinaigrette can be made several days in advance. It will keep for about one week, refrigerated.

TOASTED PECAN VINAIGRETTE

Combine sherry, vinegars, and shallot in a small saucepan over medium-high heat and bring to a boil. Reduce heat and simmer until reduced by about half the volume and shallots are soft. Cool.

Put the cooled mixture in a blender jar and add mustard and lemon juice. Blend on high speed to combine.

Very slowly, with the blender running, add the oils through the top of the blender lid to make an emulsified dressing. Remove the cover and add maple syrup, pecans, and salt and pepper. Blend until smooth. If dressing is very thick, thin with 1 to 2 teaspoons water.

Salad

3 5-ounce packages mixed baby greens or about 8 cups

1 cup cherry tomatoes, halved

½ cup pecans, toasted and chopped

8 ounces cotija cheese or a mild goat cheese, crumbled

Toasted Pecan Vinaigrette

¼ cup dry sherry

⅛ cup balsamic vinegar

¼ cup sherry vinegar

1 shallot, minced

1 teaspoon dijon mustard

2 teaspoons fresh lemon juice

½ cup light olive oil

½ cup safflower oil

2 tablespoons sugar-free maple syrup

¼ cup toasted pecans

salt and pepper to taste

NUTRITIONAL ANALYSIS (PER SALAD, WITH 1½ TABLESPOONS DRESSING)

Calories 295 (73% from fat); Protein 9 grams; Carbohydrates 7 grams; Fiber 2 grams; Fat 24 grams.

5
Soups, Stews, and Chili

Wish I had time for one more bowl of chili.
—Alleged dying words of Kit Carson

There is nothing so satisfying as a flavorful soup to start a meal or a hearty bowl of chili to make a meal. With a rich flavorful stock and zesty combinations of chiles and vegetables, soup can be as filling as it is nourishing. Chilled gazpacho on a warm summer day made with fresh ripe tomatoes, crisp cucumbers, sweet bell peppers, and fresh cilantro, or a tantalizing bowl of Black Bean Turkey Chili (p. 95) or Tortilla Soup (p. 89) topped with crisp tortilla strips can fit right into today's healthful lifestyle. The soups in this book are all low in fat, and most of them freeze well. All soups and chilies are best when made a day in advance, allowing the flavors to develop—good news for busy cooks!

TORTILLA SOUP

SERVES 8

Tortilla Soup can be a meal in itself. You may use chicken or smoked turkey, or simply serve the soup with cheese, tortilla strips, and avocado. Cooking the chicken in the soup stock gives both the stock and the chicken good flavor, but if you have leftover smoked turkey or chicken, this is a good way to use the leftovers.

Preheat an indoor or outdoor grill to the highest setting (or the middle oven rack to broil).

Rub onions and tomatoes with vegetable oil and grill on all sides until browned. Finish cooking in a 350° oven, on a cookie sheet, for about 15 to 20 minutes. Cut the tomatoes in quarters, transfer onions and tomatoes to a blender or food processor fitted with the metal blade, and blend with the chopped garlic. You may have to do this in several batches.

Put the blended tomatoes and onions in a large saucepan or stockpot. Add chicken broth and water and bring to a boil. Add chicken breasts and ancho chile pod and return to a boil. Skim the foam from the top. Reduce the heat to low and simmer, uncovered, for 25 to 30 minutes. Remove chicken and cool. Bone the meat, then shred or cut into small pieces.

In a small skillet, heat the oil and add cumin and tortillas. Stir and cook 1 to 2 minutes. Add the cumin and tortillas to the stock. Season the soup with pepper, salt, cayenne pepper, cilantro, and basil.

Simmer the soup for 10 to 15 minutes to blend the flavors. Cool. Blend the soup in several batches in a blender or food processor fitted with the metal blade.

When ready to serve, bring the soup to a boil. Adjust salt and pepper to taste. Divide the chicken among eight soup bowls. Pour the hot broth on top and garnish each bowl with 3 or 4 pieces of avocado, grated cheese, and toasted tortilla strips.

2 white onions, quartered

5 tomatoes, unpeeled, cores intact

vegetable oil

4 cloves garlic, chopped

2 14-ounce cans chicken broth

3 cups water

6 chicken breasts, bone in, fat and skin removed

1 ancho chile pod, stemmed, seeded, and toasted

1 tablespoon vegetable oil

1 teaspoon ground cumin

2 corn tortillas, cut into small pieces

½ teaspoon coarsely ground black pepper

1 teaspoon salt

pinch cayenne pepper

1 tablespoon minced fresh cilantro

1–2 tablespoons minced fresh basil

Garnishes

1 ripe but firm avocado, cut into cubes

4 ounces low-fat cheddar cheese, grated

4 corn tortillas, cut into strips and toasted

**NUTRITIONAL ANALYSIS
(PER SERVING, WITH GARNISHES)**
Calories 417 (27% from fat); Protein 48 grams;
Carbohydrates 19 grams; Fiber 4 grams; Fat 12.5 grams.

2 corn tortillas, cut into
   small pieces

1 onion, chopped

½ cup chopped yellow bell
   pepper

¾ cup chopped red bell
   pepper

1 tablespoon chili powder

2 tablespoons minced
   cilantro (optional)

1 14-ounce can beef or
   chicken broth

4 cups water

1½ cups prepared salsa or
   picante sauce

2 packages Knorr Swiss
   tomato basil soup

2 cups diced cooked chicken

1 cup white corn kernels

Garnishes

grated low-fat cheddar
   cheese

1–2 avocadoes, diced

tortilla strips

QUICK TORTILLA SOUP
SERVES 8

So many of my friends love Tortilla Soup but want an easy way to prepare it. This recipe can be done in 30 minutes, and when accompanied by a Caesar Salad, makes a satisfying light meal. You can purchase the tortilla strips from most Southwest restaurants, or bake them according to the method on page 9. I use a rotisserie chicken for the chicken and its natural juices.

Advance Preparation: The soup may be made 2 days in advance and reheated to serve. If too thick, thin as needed with chicken broth or water.

Coat a large saucepan with a vegetable-oil cooking spray. Sauté the tortillas, onion, and bell peppers until softened. Add additional spray if needed.

Sprinkle the onion mixture with the chili powder and cilantro if using and stir just to coat all the ingredients. It will thicken immediately, so add the broth and half the water, stirring constantly. Add the salsa or picante sauce and the contents of the dry soup mix and the remaining water and cook over medium-high heat, stirring constantly, until thickened. Add chicken and corn and continue cooking just to heat the chicken.

Spoon the soup into serving bowls, with garnishes on the side.

**NUTRITIONAL ANALYSIS
(PER SERVING, WITHOUT GARNISHES)**
Calories 141 (19% from fat); Protein 13 grams;
Carbohydrates 16 grams; Fiber 3 grams; Fat 3 grams.

CHICKEN LIME SOUP

MAKES 6–8 SERVINGS

This is a traditional Southwest soup that is very light and colorful.

Advance Preparation: The soup base may be prepared a day or two in advance. Add lime juice, tomatoes, avocado, and scallions when ready to serve.

Season the chicken with salt and pepper and moisten with 2 to 3 tablespoons chicken broth. Set aside.

Generously coat a 2-quart saucepan with a vegetable-oil cooking spray. Add celery, onion, and carrots and sauté 3 to 4 minutes or until softened. Add white rice, chicken broth, garlic salt, cloves, thyme, and oregano. Simmer, uncovered, for 20 to 30 minutes.

When you are ready to serve the soup, add the lime juice, tomatoes, avocado, scallions, and reserved chicken. Season to taste with salt and pepper.

Serve the soup with tortilla strips, fresh lime wedges and radishes, if using.

**NUTRITIONAL ANALYSIS
(PER SERVING, WITH GARNISHES,
BASED ON 6 SERVINGS PER RECIPE)**

Calories 275 (29% from fat); Protein 22 grams;
Carbohydrates 27 grams; Fiber 5 grams; Fat 9 grams.

---

2 chicken breasts, grilled, boned, and cut into bite-sized pieces
salt and pepper
3 14-ounce cans chicken broth
3 stalks celery, chopped
1 onion, chopped
3 carrots, chopped
4 tablespoons white rice
½ teaspoon garlic salt
¼ teaspoon ground cloves
¼ teaspoon dried thyme
½ teaspoon dried oregano

2 tablespoons fresh lime juice
2 Roma tomatoes, peeled and diced
1 avocado, peeled, pitted, and diced
8 scallions, sliced
salt and pepper

Garnishes
4 corn tortillas, cut into strips and toasted (p. 9)
lime wedges
sliced radishes (optional)

5 cups cooked Black Beans
(p. 16)

1 14-ounce can chicken
broth

1 4½-ounce can green chiles

1 jalapeño chile, stemmed
and seeded

1 8-ounce can tomato sauce

2–4 tablespoons dry sherry

½–1 teaspoon salt

Garnishes

3 ounces grated Monterey
jack cheese

sliced scallions, green and
white part

Pico de Gallo (p. 28) or
fresh diced tomatoes

Chile Poblano Cream
(p. 40) or non-fat sour
cream

BLACK BEAN SOUP
MAKES ABOUT 7 CUPS, SERVES 6

Always a favorite, this soup is hearty enough to make a meal when served with a salad or soft tacos. Choose from any of the suggested garnishes or combine several for a colorful presentation. If you use Smoked Turkey Stock (p. 14), it will give the soup a rich, smoky flavor.

Advance Preparation: The soup may be prepared a day in advance. It may be necessary to add a little chicken stock when reheating.

Using a food processor fitted with the metal blade or a blender, blend the beans with ½ to 1 cup of the chicken broth, green chiles, jalapeño, and tomato sauce. You may have to do this in several batches.

Heat the blended beans with the remaining chicken broth and sherry in a large saucepan over medium heat, stirring occasionally, until hot. Season to taste with salt. Ladle into warm soup bowls. Serve the soup with bowls of garnish on the side.

If using Chile Poblano Cream or sour cream as a garnish, put it in a plastic squirt bottle or in a small resealable bag. Snip the corner with scissors and then drizzle cream on the hot soup.

**NUTRITIONAL ANALYSIS
(PER SERVING, WITHOUT GARNISHES)**
Calories 218 (4% from fat); Protein 14 grams;
Carbohydrates 38 grams; Fiber 13 grams; Fat 1 gram.

SHRIMP GAZPACHO

SERVES 6

This is just as good without the shrimp (and lower in calories). It's almost fat-free, very low in calories, and full of flavor.

Advance Preparation: The soup may be prepared a day in advance. Add the shrimp before serving.

If Texas sweet onions are not available, use a sweet red onion. Cut into 6 pieces and soak in ice water 15 minutes before blending.

Using a blender or food processor fitted with the metal blade, blend the onion, garlic, and tomatoes. Set aside ½ cup each of the cucumber and red bell pepper. Blend the remaining cucumber and red bell pepper along with serrano chiles and vinegar. Add 1 cup of the tomato juice, tomato paste, parsley, basil, and salt. (You will have to do this in several batches.)

Transfer the blended vegetables to a large bowl. Add remaining tomato juice. Stir in green bell pepper, shrimp, and reserved cucumber and red bell pepper. Season with salt and pepper. Chill 2 hours before serving.

Divide gazpacho among 6 bowls and garnish each with a lime wedge and toasted tortillas.

**NUTRITIONAL ANALYSIS
(PER SERVING, WITHOUT GARNISH)**
Calories 125 (% from fat); Protein 11 grams;
Carbohydrates 18 grams; Fiber 3 grams; Fat 1 gram.

½ sweet Texas onion

2 cloves garlic, sliced

4 ripe tomatoes, peeled, cored, and quartered

2 small cucumbers, seeded, peeled and cut into chunks

1 red bell pepper, diced

2 serrano chiles, stemmed and seeded

¼ cup red wine vinegar

4 cups tomato or tomato/vegetable juice

2 tablespoons tomato paste

2 sprigs each parsley and basil

½ teaspoon salt

½ cup diced green bell pepper

½ pound cooked shrimp, chopped coarsely

salt and pepper

Garnishes
6 lime wedges
thin tortilla strips, toasted

1 large zucchini, sliced lengthwise into 4 strips

1 large yellow squash, sliced lengthwise into 4 strips

2 ears fresh corn, husks removed

salt and pepper

1 large turnip, peeled and diced

1 large onion, chopped

2 carrots, peeled and diced

2 14-ounce cans chicken or vegetable broth

1 16-ounce can Mexican-style diced tomatoes, tomatoes chopped

1 green bell pepper, diced

1 red bell pepper, diced

3 cups diced cooked chicken (optional)

1 cup cooked pinto beans (optional)

½ teaspoon salt

¼ teaspoon coarsely ground black pepper

1 tablespoon fresh minced cilantro

2 cups julienned spinach, uncooked

Garnishes

toasted tortilla strips

lime wedges

ROASTED CORN AND GRILLED VEGETABLE SOUP

SERVES 8

The grilled vegetables add a rich flavor to this low-fat vegetable soup. Add cooked chicken or pinto beans to make a more substantial soup.

To cook the squashes and corn, heat the grill to the highest setting. Coat the vegetables with a vegetable-oil cooking spray and place them on the grill. Season with salt and pepper and grill on both sides until just tender. Cool and cut both squashes into ¼-inch dice. Cut corn from the cob and set aside.

Place a large saucepan over medium heat. Coat generously with a vegetable-oil cooking spray and sauté the turnip, onion, and carrots 3 to 4 minutes. Season with salt and pepper, turning often. Add about 1 cup of the chicken or vegetable broth and bring to a boil. Simmer 3 to 5 minutes, then add remaining broth and tomatoes.

Add bell peppers, squash, and corn and simmer until peppers are softened, about 5 to 6 minutes. Add chicken and beans if using and heat through. Add salt, pepper, and cilantro to taste.

Add the spinach just prior to serving or place spinach in each serving bowl and pour the hot soup on top.

Garnish with toasted tortillas and lime wedges.

NUTRITIONAL ANALYSIS
(PER SERVING, WITHOUT GARNISH)
Calories 201 (16% from fat); Protein 22 grams;
Carbohydrates 21 grams; Fiber 6 grams; Fat 3.5 grams.

BLACK BEAN TURKEY CHILI

SERVES 10

An answer to leftover turkey, this chili makes a good buffet dish for your winter football get-togethers. You may use canned green chiles in place of poblano chiles; however, the flavor and color of poblano chiles are superior.

Heat the safflower oil over medium heat in a 6-quart saucepan. Add the onions and garlic and sauté until softened, about 5 minutes. Stir in the chiles, peppers, chili powder, and cumin.

Add the chicken broth and cook 25 to 30 minutes. Add turkey, corn, and black beans to the broth. Stir in salt, pepper, and cornmeal and simmer 10 to 15 minutes.

Serve with bowls of garnish and warm corn tortillas or corn muffins.

**NUTRITIONAL ANALYSIS
(PER SERVING, WITHOUT GARNISH)**
Calories 248 (22% from fat); Protein 31 grams;
Carbohydrates 17 grams; Fiber 5 grams; Fat 6 grams.

---

1 tablespoon safflower oil

1 red onion, diced

1 white onion, diced

4 cloves garlic, minced

4 poblano chiles, roasted, peeled, and diced

1 red bell pepper, roasted, peeled, and diced

2 cups diced green bell pepper

⅓ cup chili powder

1 teaspoon ground cumin

7–8 cups chicken broth

2 pounds turkey meat, diced

1 cup corn kernels

1 cup cooked black beans, liquid drained

½–1 teaspoon salt

½ teaspoon black pepper

1 tablespoon cornmeal

Garnishes
green onions, sliced

thinly sliced radishes

non-fat sour cream

low-fat cheese, grated

1¼ pounds top round, coarsely ground

1 large onion, chopped

1 large green or red bell pepper, diced

6 tablespoons chili powder

½ teaspoon ground cumin

1 14½-ounce can diced tomatoes, including juices, puréed, or 2 8-ounce cans tomato sauce

2 tablespoons cornmeal

1 fresh poblano chile, roasted, peeled, and diced (optional)

2 14-ounce cans beef broth

1 tablespoon apple cider vinegar

½ teaspoon dried oregano

½–1 teaspoon salt

fresh cracked black pepper

1 14½-ounce can pinto beans, including liquid (optional)

Garnishes

1 bunch scallions, sliced

low-fat grated cheese

CHILI CON CARNE
SERVES 8

Fresh poblano chiles will add delicious flavor to the chili (no fat and minimal calories) and are well worth the trouble. You may substitute ground turkey for the beef with surprisingly good results. Venison is also a good choice if ground without added fat.

Coat a 4-quart saucepan with vegetable-oil cooking spray and place over medium-high heat. Add the beef and sear, without stirring, until browned. Break up the meat with a fork and cook 3 to 4 minutes, stirring until juices no longer run pink. Place the meat in a strainer set over a bowl and press to strain the juices. Place the bowl in the freezer to solidify fat for easy removal.

Return the meat to the same pan, add onion and bell pepper, and continue cooking over medium-high heat. Stir in chili powder and cumin, then add tomatoes or tomato sauce and cornmeal. Continue to stir, adding poblano chile, if using. Simmer the chili over medium-low heat for 30 minutes, stirring occasionally.

Remove the bowl from the freezer. Remove and discard the solid fat from the top of the reserved juices. Add the thawed beef broth, canned beef broth, vinegar, oregano, salt, and pepper to the chili. If using beans, add them now. Heat thoroughly and adjust salt and pepper to taste.

Serve the chili with bowls of sliced scallions and low-fat grated cheese.

NUTRITIONAL ANALYSIS (PER SERVING WITHOUT PINTO BEANS OR GARNISHES)
Calories 243 (46% from fat); Protein 22 grams;
Carbohydrates 10 grams; Fiber ; Fat 12.5 grams.

NUTRITIONAL ANALYSIS (PER SERVING WITH PINTO BEANS, WITHOUT GARNISHES)
Calories 297 (39% from fat); Protein 25 grams;
Carbohydrates 20 grams; Fiber 7 grams; Fat 13 grams.

CHICKEN CHILI

SERVES 8

This low-fat, low-carb version of a white bean and chicken chili recipe has been passed around for several years. This version is a good dish for entertaining that can be paired with Chili con Carne (p. 96) and a Caesar Salad (p. 72). The chili is best made a day ahead and reheated.

While beans are low in fat, they do add significantly to carb count, so I have omitted them.

In a medium to large stockpot, heat the olive oil and sauté garlic, onion, and bell pepper for 3 to 4 minutes.

Add water, chicken broth, and lemon pepper and bring to a boil. Add chicken, return to a boil, then reduce the heat to a simmer, cover, and cook about 20 minutes Remove the chicken (reserving the broth and vegetables). Trim the chicken from the bone and cut the breast meat into bite-sized pieces. Set aside.

Add green chiles, cumin, lime juice, and chicken to the broth. Season with salt and pepper. Return to a boil, then cool completely and refrigerate overnight.

When ready to serve, add corn, if using, heat through, and season with salt and pepper. Garnish the chili with Pico de Gallo and grated cheese.

1 tablespoon olive oil

3 garlic cloves

1 large yellow onion, chopped

2 yellow bell peppers, diced

½ cup water

3 14-ounce cans chicken broth

1 tablespoon lemon pepper

6 chicken breasts, bone in, skin and fat trimmed

2 4½-ounce cans diced green chiles

1 teaspoon ground cumin

3 tablespoons fresh lime juice

salt and pepper

1 cup white corn kernels (optional)

Garnishes

Pico de Gallo (p. 28)

grated Monterey jack or Manchego cheese

NUTRITIONAL ANALYSIS (PER SERVING WITH CORN, WITHOUT GARNISHES)

Calories 283 (22% from fat); Protein 43 grams;
Carbohydrates 12 grams; Fiber 2 grams; Fat 7 grams.

1½ pounds lean ground round or turkey

1½ onions, chopped

1½ tablespoons chili powder

½ envelope ranch dressing mix

2 cups chicken or beef broth

1 14½-ounce can diced tomatoes

2 4½-ounce cans diced green chiles

½ cup hominy or corn kernels

½ 14 ½-ounce can ranch style pinto beans (optional)

1 pound light American processed cheese

TACO SOUP

SERVES 6

There are many versions of this popular soup, but most are pretty high in both fat and carbs. I have removed the beans, reduced the hominy, and used a light cheese. It's still a delicious combination of flavors.

Coat a medium to large saucepan with a vegetable-oil cooking spray. Add ground beef or turkey and onion, and sauté until browned. Add chili powder while the meat is cooking, but do not break the meat into a fine mixture. You do want "clumps" of meat.

When the meat is cooked, add the ranch dressing seasoning, chicken or beef broth, tomatoes, green chiles, and hominy or corn, and pinto beans if using. Bring to a simmer and, stirring constantly, gradually add the cheese. Stir until all the cheese is melted.

Serve the soup with a simple salad.

**NUTRITIONAL ANALYSIS
(PER SERVING WITHOUT BEANS)**

Calories 356 (48% from fat); Protein 30 grams;
Carbohydrates 16 grams; Fiber 2 grams; Fat 19 grams.

**NUTRITIONAL ANALYSIS
(PER SERVING WITH BEANS)**

Calories 403 (47% from fat); Protein 33 grams;
Carbohydrates 25 grams; Fiber 6 grams; Fat 19 grams.

Decadent Chocolate Cake (p. 197) with Tequila Sabayon (p. 198).

Top: Los Cabos Shrimp Cocktail (p. 54), Shrimp and Scallop Ceviche (p. 53), and Salmon and Scallop Ceviche (p. 52).

Pecan Crusted Sea Bass (p. 119) with Spaghetti Squash (p. 120) and Roasted Bell Pepper Sauce (p. 127).

Roasted Halibut with Pico de Gallo Vinaigrette (p. 113) and Wild Pecan Rice (p. 178).

Barbecue Chicken Salad (p. 85), Spicy Crab Tortilla Bites (p. 66), Smoked Salmon Tortilla Bites (p. 65), and Pimiento Cheese Roll Ups (p. 62).

Simple Grilled Salmon (p. 115) with Cilantro Cream (p. 118) and Seared Spinich (p. 171).

Lettuce Wrap Tacos (p. 145) and (mini) Fish Tacos (p. 142).

Braised Pork Tenderloin with Chipotle Whiskey Sauce (p. 135), Oven Roasted Asparagus (p. 172), Chipotle Mashed Sweet Potatoes (p. 176), and Simple Mixed Green Salad (p. 87).

CREAMY CORN SOUP

MAKES 8 1-CUP SERVINGS

This creamy soup is made without cream and makes a delicious base that you can be creative with. You can add diced sautéed vegetables or cooked shellfish. Use any of the suggested garnishes to add color flavor. The soup can be served hot or chilled.

In a large saucepan, heat the water and chicken broth. Place the corn cobs on a cutting board and using a sharp knife, cut corn kernels from the cob. You can cut very close, cutting away some of the cob. Add both the cobs and the corn to the saucepan and bring to a boil. Maintain a simmer.

Coat a skillet with vegetable-oil cooking spray. Add the onion, garlic, and shallot and sauté until softened. Add to the broth, cover and simmer for 40 minutes. Cool completely.

Remove corn cobs and discard. Using a blender, blend the contents of the saucepan and cream style corn in several batches. Strain, pressing to extract as much liquid as possible. Discard corn pulp

Put the cream cheese in the blender and blend with 1 cup of the corn liquid until smooth. Put the cream cheese and all the strained corn liquid back in the saucepan and season with cayenne pepper, salt, and peper. Return to a simmer.

If you want thicker soup, dissolve 2 tablespoons of cornstarch with about 1 cup of the soup, stir until smooth, and then add to the soup, stirring constantly until the soup reaches a simmer.

If adding shellfish, add cooked shellfish while reheating the soup.

Serve soup with garnishes of choice.

4 cups of water

1 14 ounce can chicken broth

5 ears fresh corn

1 large onion, coarsely chopped

2 cloves fresh garlic

1 shallot, halved

1 15-ounce can cream style corn

4 ounces light or low-fat cream cheese

¼ teaspoon cayenne pepper

salt and pepper to taste

Garnishes

snipped chives or

sliced scallions and sun-dried tomatoes or Chile Poblano Cream (p. 40)

NUTRITIONAL ANALYSIS (PER SERVING)

Calories 108 (25% from fat); Protein 4 grams;
Carbohydrates 18 grams; Fiber 1 gram; Fat 3 grams.

6
Main Dishes

The discovery of a new dish does more for the happiness of man than the discovery of a star.

—Brillat-Savarin, French gastronome

Where or when the first platter of sizzling fajitas started is a topic for heated discussion, but one thing everyone agrees on is that their instant popularity spread like wild fire. Freshly grilled meats, chicken, pan-seared onions and peppers, with warm, soft tortillas, pico de gallo, and guacamole have universal appeal. When prepared at home, fajitas can be a light, healthful meal.

Light entrées in this section are not limited to fajitas. Red Snapper Veracruz (p. 107), a classic Mexican dish, makes cooking fish as easy as it is light. Other seafood entrées are grilled or oven roasted and rely on assertive marinades, warm salsas, light vinaigrettes, or a spicy glaze for added flavor and zest.

Chicken Margarita (p. 124) is marinated in tequila and lime, which both tenderizes and flavors. Halibut is oven-roasted with spicy chile pesto and fresh, sweet tomatoes. Skinless chicken breast is crusted with cornbread crumbs and a sprinkling of pecans to make an entrée that defies its low fat grams.

Some advance preparation is possible in all the main dishes, making them suitable for entertaining. Seafood and shellfish are emphasized to keep the main entrée on the lighter side and to save some room for appetizers and desserts!

FAJITAS

The popularity of this dish is due in no small measure to the "sizzling" presentation popularized by restaurants. Fajitas are no longer limited to beef and chicken. Pork, shrimp, catfish, vegetables—even apple pie—are served on sizzling platters.

The marinade that follows can be used for beef, chicken, and fish. Sizzling Sauce (p.103) is great for reheating fajitas. The good thing about fajitas is you can make all the accompaniments (p. 112) in advance and have everything done before your guests arrive. Be aware of the amount of sour cream, cheese, and guacamole you add to each tortilla—that's where the fat and calories add up.

If you serve fajitas with onions and peppers, put both on the sizzling platter, side by side.

For all fajitas, fat grams and calories are for meat, poultry, shrimp, or vegetables only. Add fat grams and calories for each corn or flour tortilla as well as the accompaniments. If you want to almost eliminate carbs, serve fajitas with a choice of tortillas or lettuce "wraps."

MARINADE

Combine the marinade ingredients: garlic, lime juice, chiles, Worcestershire sauce, onion, wine, pepper, and safflower oil.

Marinade will keep for one week but should be discarded after used with beef, chicken, or fish. The marinade is only minimally absorbed and does not significantly alter nutritional data.

Marinade

6 cloves garlic, minced

⅓ cup fresh lime juice

2 jalapeño chiles, chopped

3 tablespoons Worcestershire sauce

½ cup chopped onion

½ cup white wine

½ tablespoon coarsely ground black pepper

2 cups safflower oil

2½ pounds top round or
flank steak

salt and pepper

BEEF FAJITAS

SERVES 6, TWO WRAPS PER PERSON

Trim the meat of all visible fat. Lightly pound with a meat tenderizer to an even thickness. Marinate 3 to 4 hours, covered and refrigerated.

Heat an outdoor grill to make a hot fire. Remove the meat from the marinade and season with salt and pepper. Grill on both sides over the hot fire about 2 minutes per side. Cover and set aside.

Heat the Sizzling Sauce (p. 103) in a small pan. Cut the meat into thin strips. Place an iron skillet over high heat. Add a few drops of oil and stir-fry the meat a few seconds to reheat. Drizzle with Sizzling Sauce, and serve with warm flour tortillas and accompaniments.

**NUTRITIONAL ANALYSIS
(PER SERVING TOP ROUND ONLY)**

Calories 362 (37% from fat); Protein 53 grams; Carbohydrates less than 1 gram; Fiber less than 1 gram; Fat 15 grams.

**NUTRITIONAL ANALYSIS
(PER SERVING FLANK STEAK ONLY)**

Calories 351 (44% from fat); Protein 49 grams; Carbohydrates less than 1 gram; Fiber less than 1 gram; Fat 17 grams.

ACCOMPANIMENTS

Prepare accompaniments of choice and arrange on a platter to serve with fajitas. Sizzle onions and peppers with the meat.

SIZZLING SAUCE

> **NUTRITIONAL ANALYSIS**
> **(SIZZLING SAUCE, PER TABLESPOON)**
> Calories 13 (63% from fat); Protein less than 1 gram;
> Carbohydrates less than 1 gram; Fiber less than 1 gram;
> Fat less than 1 gram

ONIONS AND PEPPERS

SERVES 4

Place a large skillet over medium heat. Coat with a vegetable-oil cooking spray. Add the onion and peppers and stir-fry until lightly browned. Season with salt and pepper. Serve with beef, chicken, or shrimp fajitas.

> **NUTRITIONAL ANALYSIS (PER SERVING)**
> Calories 49 (7% from fat); Protein 1 gram;
> Carbohydrates 11 grams; Fiber 2 grams; Fat less than 1 gram.

Accompaniments

1 head thinly sliced romaine lettuce

Skinny Guacamole (p. 44)

Pico de Gallo (p. 28)

1 cup light sour cream

8 ounces low-fat cheddar cheese, grated

fresh lime wedges

corn or flour tortillas or warmed pita halves

Grilled Onions and Peppers

Sizzling Sauce

½ cup chicken or beef broth

3 tablespoons soy sauce

2 tablespoons light butter, melted

¼ cup white wine

Onions and Peppers

1 onion, cut into julienne strips

1 red bell pepper, cut into julienne strips

1 yellow bell pepper, cut into julienne strips

1 green bell pepper, cut into julienne strips

salt and pepper

8 large skinless boneless
chicken breast halves

salt and pepper

CHICKEN FAJITAS

SERVES 8, 2 WRAPS PER PERSON

Combine the marinade ingredients (p. 101): garlic, lime juice, chiles, Worcestershire sauce, onion, wine, pepper, and safflower oil. Trim visible fat from the chicken and lightly pound to an even thickness with a meat tenderizer. Marinate 2 to 3 hours, covered and refrigerated. Remove chicken from marinade and discard the marinade.

Season the chicken with salt and pepper and grill over a hot fire about 1½ minutes per side. Remove, cover, and set aside.

Heat the Sizzling Sauce (p. 103) in a small pan. Cut the chicken into thin strips. Place an iron skillet over high heat. Add a few drops of oil and stir-fry the chicken strips a few seconds to reheat. Drizzle with Sizzling Sauce and serve with warm flour tortillas and accompaniments (p. 103).

NUTRITIONAL ANALYSIS
(PER SERVING CHICKEN ONLY)

Calories 302 (30% from fat); Protein 53 grams; Carbohydrates less than 1 gram; Fiber less than 1 gram; Fat 10 grams.

SHRIMP FAJITAS

SERVES 6, 2 WRAPS PER PERSON

Combine the marinade ingredients (p. 101): garlic, lime juice, chiles, Worcestershire sauce, onion, wine, pepper, and safflower oil. Stir the fresh cilantro into the marinade. Peel and devein the shrimp and remove tails. Marinate 30 minutes.

Skewer shrimp on wooden skewers that have been soaked in water. Brush with olive oil and season with coarse salt and lemon pepper. Grill over a hot fire about 1 minute per side. Cool, then cut shrimp in half to make thin slices.

Heat the Sizzling Sauce (p. 103) in a small pan. Place an iron skillet over medium heat. Add a few drops of oil and stir-fry the shrimp a few seconds to reheat. Drizzle with Sizzling Sauce and serve with warm flour tortillas and accompaniments (p. 103).

2 tablespoons fresh cilantro

2 pounds large shrimp
  (21–25 count)

olive oil

coarse salt

lemon pepper

**NUTRITIONAL ANALYSIS
(PER SERVING SHRIMP ONLY)**

Calories 180 (25% from fat); Protein 33 grams;
Carbohydrates 1 gram; Fiber less than 1 gram; Fat 5 grams.

---

2 carrots, diagonally sliced

2 yellow squash, diagonally
   sliced

2 zucchini, diagonally sliced

10 large mushrooms, halved

1 red bell pepper

1 yellow bell pepper

1 green bell pepper

1 bunch scallion, white part
   only

12 cherry tomatoes

olive oil or safflower oil

salt and pepper

VEGETABLE FAJITAS

SERVES 4

Blanch the carrots in boiling salted water for 1 minute.

It is not necessary to marinate the vegetables; simply brush with olive or safflower oil and season with salt and pepper. Grill over a hot fire until well marked and just tender. Cut the squashes and peppers into strips.

Place the vegetables in a heated fajita skillet or sizzle pan and drizzle with a small amount of Sizzling Sauce (p. 103). Serve with tortillas and accompaniments (p. 103, except onions and peppers).

**NUTRITIONAL ANALYSIS
(PER SERVING VEGETABLES ONLY)**

Calories 140 (26% from fat); Protein 6 grams;
Carbohydrates 20 grams; Fiber 4 grams; Fat 4 grams.

RED SNAPPER VERACRUZ

SERVES 6

Almost any flaky white fish may be used for this dish. Choose from halibut, grouper, flounder, or redfish. This is a good dish for entertaining and a foolproof way to cook fish at home. Serve the snapper with grilled vegetables or a simple salad with shredded lettuce, diced tomatoes, and toasted tortilla strips.

Advance Preparation: The sauce may be made a day in advance and reheated.

Preheat the oven to 375°.

Place the fish in a 9 × 13 baking dish and season with salt and pepper.

Pour the lime juice and orange juice over the fillets.

To make the sauce, heat the oil in a large skillet over medium heat and sauté the garlic, onion, and bell pepper until translucent. Add the diced tomatoes and poblano chiles and bring the sauce to a simmer. Stir in the vinegar, olives, capers, tomato sauce, salt, pepper, and cilantro and remove from the heat.

Spoon the sauce over the fish and bake, uncovered, at 375° for 8 minutes. Cover loosely with foil and bake an additional 4 to 6 minutes. Remove the fish with a spatula to heated serving plates. Transfer the sauce to a saucepan and bring to a boil, stirring constantly.

Spoon the sauce on each fillet and garnish with fresh minced parsley. Serve pickled jalapeños on the side.

6 8-ounce halibut, grouper, flounder, or redfish fillets

salt and pepper

2 fresh limes

juice from ½ orange

1 tablespoon safflower oil

2 cloves garlic, minced

1 red onion, thinly sliced

½ green bell pepper, cut into short julienne strips

1 14½-ounce can Mexican-style diced tomatoes

2 large poblano chiles, roasted, peeled, and cut into short julienne strips

1 tablespoon red wine vinegar

10 pitted black olives, sliced

3 tablespoons capers

1 8-ounce can tomato sauce

½–1 teaspoon salt

¼ teaspoon coarsely ground black pepper

1 tablespoon minced cilantro

Garnishes

minced fresh parsley

pickled jalapeño chiles

NUTRITIONAL ANALYSIS
(PER SERVING, MADE WITH RED SNAPPER)

Calories 372 (18% from fat); Protein 64 grams;
Carbohydrates 12 grams; Fiber 3 grams; Fat 7.5 grams.

6 8-ounce red snapper fillets

safflower or olive oil

salt and pepper

Warm Shrimp Salsa

1 tablespoon light butter

1 tablespoon safflower oil

2 shallots, minced

1 clove garlic, minced

1½ cups coarsely chopped
shrimp, peeled and
deveined

¼ cup rice wine vinegar

juice from ½ lemon

2 serrano chiles, stemmed,
seeded, and diced

1 cup peeled, diced
tomatoes

1 small avocado, diced

½ cup diced mango

1 tablespoon fresh cilantro

salt and pepper

Garnish

several sprigs of fresh
cilantro

GRILLED RED SNAPPER WITH WARM SHRIMP SALSA

SERVES 6

I've also prepared this recipe with fresh jumbo lump crabmeat, when in season, with excellent results. The ingredients and methods are the same; however, the crab requires less cooking time because it is already cooked.

Preheat the grill to make a hot fire.

Coat the fillets with oil on both sides and season with salt and pepper. Rub the grill with an oil-dampened rag to prevent the fish from sticking. Grill the fillets on one side about 5 minutes. Using a spatula, carefully turn the fish and grill on the opposite side about 3 minutes. Allow 7 to 8 minutes per 1-inch thickness of fish. Remove the fillets to a plate, cover, and keep warm while preparing the Warm Shrimp Salsa.

**NUTRITIONAL ANALYSIS
(PER SERVING, WITHOUT SALSA)**

Calories 322 (23% from fat); Protein 62 grams; Carbohydrates less than 1 gram; Fiber less than 1 gram; Fat 8.5 grams.

WARM SHRIMP SALSA

Heat the butter and oil in a medium skillet over medium heat. Add the shallots, garlic, and shrimp. Sauté 2 to 3 minutes or until the shrimp turns pink.

Add the vinegar, lemon juice, Serrano chiles, and tomatoes. Cook just long enough to heat the tomatoes and combine ingredients. Remove from heat and gently stir in avocado and cilantro. Season with salt and pepper. Spoon Warm Shrimp Salsa over grilled fish and garnish with several sprigs of fresh cilantro.

**NUTRITIONAL ANALYSIS (PER ¾ CUP,
BASED ON 4½ CUPS PER RECIPE)**

Calories 140 (58% from fat); Protein 8 grams;
Carbohydrates 7 grams; Fiber 2 gram; Fat 9 grams.

GRILLED SWORDFISH WITH TEQUILA LIME VINAIGRETTE

SERVES 6

Grilled swordfish or tuna may be served with any of the salsas in this book. Tequila Lime Vinaigrette (p. 110), a simple reduction of citrus and tequila, makes the base for a "salsa" vinaigrette that is both colorful and delicious with grilled fish.

Prepare a gas or charcoal grill and preheat to make a hot fire. Brush the grill with an oil-dampened cloth to prevent the fish from sticking.

In a blender combine the garlic, shallots, serrano chiles, and cilantro. Blend on high speed. Add the oil and salt and set aside. This is the basting sauce.

Trim dark meat from the swordfish and remove skin. Put the swordfish on a platter and brush both sides with the basting sauce.

Place the fish on the grill, season with salt and pepper, and grill 5 minutes. Turn and grill on the opposite side and cook about 3 minutes. Allow about 7 to 8 minutes total time per 1-inch thickness of the fish.

Ladle Tequila Lime Vinaigrette on top of each steak. Garnish with fresh basil.

Basting Sauce
2 garlic cloves
2 shallots
3 serrano chiles
½ cup cilantro sprigs
¾ cup safflower or olive oil
½ teaspoon coarse salt

6 8-ounce swordfish steaks

salt and pepper

Garnish
sprig of fresh basil

NUTRITIONAL ANALYSIS
(PER SERVING, WITHOUT VINAIGRETTE)
Calories 366 (49% from fat); Protein 45 grams; Carbohydrates less than 1 gram; Fiber less than 1 gram; Fat 20 grams.

Vinaigrette

⅓ cup tequila

2 tablespoons Triple Sec

¼ cup fresh lemon juice

¼ cup fresh lime juice

1 shallot, minced

1 garlic clove, minced

2 tablespoons rice wine
  vinegar

2 tablespoons safflower oil

⅓ cup finely diced mango

⅓ cup finely diced, roasted,
  and peeled red bell
  pepper

½ tablespoon minced fresh
  basil

½ tablespoon minced fresh
  cilantro

salt and pepper

TEQUILA LIME VINAIGRETTE

Put tequila, Triple Sec, lemon juice, lime juice, shallot, garlic, and vinegar in a small pan over high heat. Bring to a boil and reduce the liquid by half of the original volume. Remove from the heat and whisk in the oil. Add the mango, red bell pepper, basil, and cilantro. Season with salt and pepper.

**NUTRITIONAL ANALYSIS
(2 TABLESPOONS PER SERVING)**

Calories 36 (50% from fat); Protein 1 gram;
Carbohydrates 2 grams; Fiber less than 1 gram; Fat 2 grams.

PESTO ROASTED HALIBUT

SERVES 4

This combination of textures and flavors gives a mild fish a new personality. While the pesto is spicy by itself, the combination is not hot—just flavorful. The Yellow Bell Pepper Sauce may be made with red or yellow bell peppers and complements both the pesto and the fish. You may also use swordfish, red snapper, orange roughy, or flounder.

Advance Preparation: Both the sauce and the pesto may be made a day in advance.

Preheat the oven to 400°.

Coat the fish with an olive-oil cooking spray and season with salt and pepper. Place fillets in a roasting pan, and add 1 cup each white wine and water. The fillets should not be submerged in the liquid. Spread about 1 tablespoon pesto over each fillet and drizzle with butter. Roast for 5 minutes, then top each fillet with diced tomatoes and cook an additional 5 to 8 minutes or until fish flakes easily with a fork.

Ladle one-fourth the Yellow Bell Pepper Sauce onto each serving plate, covering the entire plate. Put several spears of Oven-Roasted Asparagus in the middle with the halibut on top. Garnish with fresh cilantro.

4 8-ounce halibut fillets

salt and pepper

1 cup white wine

1 cup water

Spicy Green Chile Pesto
  (p. 20)

2 tablespoons light butter,
  melted

1 cup diced tomatoes

Accompaniment

Yellow Bell Pepper Sauce
  (p. 112)

Oven-Roasted Asparagus
  (p. 172)

Garnish

several sprigs of fresh
  cilantro

NUTRITIONAL ANALYSIS
(PER SERVING, WITHOUT SAUCE)

Calories 405 (47% from fat); Protein 50 grams;
Carbohydrates 4 grams; Fiber less than 1 gram; Fat 21 grams.

Sauce

2 large yellow bell peppers, roasted and peeled

1 large shallot, minced

2 cloves garlic, minced

¼ cup white wine

juice from ½ lemon

½ cup chicken broth

1 tablespoon cornstarch

1½ ounces light or low-fat cream cheese

salt and pepper

YELLOW BELL PEPPER SAUCE

Cut the peppers into small pieces and place in a blender jar. Add all accumulated juices from the peppers. Blend to chop.

In a small saucepan heat the shallot and garlic in white wine over medium heat for a few minutes or until garlic is softened. Add to the blender jar and blend with the peppers until smooth. Add lemon juice, chicken broth, cornstarch, and cream cheese and blend on high to mix well. Pour the blended mixture into a small saucepan over medium heat and stir constantly for 3 to 4 minutes or until the sauce is thickened and hot. Season with salt and pepper. If the sauce is not completely smooth, blend again.

NUTRITIONAL ANALYSIS (PER SERVING)

Calories 67 (34% from fat); Protein 3 grams;
Carbohydrates 8 grams; Fiber 1 gram; Fat 2.5 grams.

ROASTED HALIBUT WITH PICO DE GALLO VINAIGRETTE

SERVES 6 (WITH PESTO)

This is an easy way to prepare fish for a party. The light vinaigrette is also excellent with grilled swordfish, salmon, or a simple grilled chicken breast. Use the greater amount of jalapeño for a spicier sauce. Serve the fish on Wild Pecan Rice or the Cornmeal Pudding. If you can get yellow tomatoes, a combination of red and yellow tomatoes makes a very colorful dish.

You may also cook halibut on a cedar or alderwood plank, see p. 116–17 for instructions.

Preheat the oven to 350°.

Brush the halibut fillets with olive oil and season with salt and pepper. Place fillets on a baking sheet that has been sprayed with an olive-oil cooking spray. Spoon a few of the tomatoes from the vinaigrette over the fish and top evenly with Parmesan cheese. Bake about 15 to 20 minutes, or until the fish flakes easily with a fork. Don't use the liquid from the vinaigrette, or the fish could become mushy. Cooking time varies with the thickness of the fish. Drizzle a small amount of melted butter over each filet.

Warm the remaining vinaigrette in a small skillet over medium heat. Serve the halibut on Wild Pecan Rice or Cornmeal Pudding and spoon warmed vinaigrette over the top.

**NUTRITIONAL ANALYSIS
(PER SERVING WITH CILANTRO PESTO)**

Calories 272 (20% from fat); Protein 46 grams; Carbohydrates less than 1 gram; Fiber less than 1 gram; Fat 9 grams.

---

low-fat, low-carb

6 7–8 ounce halibut fillets, 1½ inches thick

olive oil

salt and pepper

Suggested Accompaniment

Wild Pecan Rice (p. 178) or Cornmeal Pudding (p. 180)

2 cups quartered cherry or
teardrop tomatoes or
diced red and yellow
tomatoes

1–2 jalapeño chiles,
stemmed, seeded, and
diced

6 scallions, trimmed and
sliced thin

3 tablespoons fresh lemon
juice

2 tablespoons fresh orange
juice

4 tablespoons light olive oil

1 tablespoon fresh minced
basil

2 tablespoons grated
Parmesan cheese

2 tablespoons light butter

salt and pepper

Note: If desired, you
can use a tablespoon
of basil pesto in place
of minced basil to finish
the vinaigrette.

PICO DE GALLO
VINAIGRETTE

Combine the tomatoes and their juices with the jalapeño in a
glass bowl. Stir in scallions, lemon juice, orange juice, olive oil,
and fresh basil. Season with salt and pepper. Bring to room
temperature before using.

**NUTRITIONAL ANALYSIS (PER ½ CUP,
BASED ON 3 CUPS PER RECIPE)**

Calories 103 (% from fat); Protein less than 1 gram;
Carbohydrates 5 grams; Fiber 1 gram; Fat 9 grams.

SIMPLE GRILLED SALMON

SERVES 6

By grilling the salmon over a hot fire, the natural juices are sealed in so the fish needs little sauce. Serve it on Seared Spinach with fresh lemon wedges or drizzle with Cilantro Cream as an accent sauce. If you like to marinate salmon, try the Margarita Marinade (p. 124) or use a low-calorie Italian dressing. In both cases, marinate only 10 to 12 minutes, refrigerated.

Be sure to ask the butcher to remove the skin. "Skin side down" refers to where the skin was removed.

Squeeze lemon juice over the salmon filets and let stand at room temperature 8 minutes. Discard lemon juice.

Brush the grill with oil to help prevent sticking. Be sure the grill is clean.

Preheat the grill on high heat. Brush the salmon with olive oil and season with salt and pepper. Place skin side down in the center of the grill and grill covered, for 5 minutes. Brush again with olive oil, turn, and grill on the opposite side for 12 to 15 minutes.

Meanwhile, prepare the Seared Spinach. This takes about 5 minutes. Divide the spinach between 6 serving plates. Remove the salmon from the grill, carefully peeling away the loosened skin, if the butcher hasn't done so prior. Turn the salmon over and place on the spinach.

Serve with lemon wedges, or drizzle a small amount of Cilantro Cream over the top.

6 8-ounce salmon fillets, about 1 inch thick in the center
juice from 2 lemons
olive oil
salt and pepper

Seared Spinach (p. 171)

Garnishes
lemon wedges
Cilantro Cream (p. 22)

NUTRITIONAL ANALYSIS
(PER SERVING, WITHOUT GARNISHES)

Calories 500 (47% from fat); Protein 64 grams;
Carbohydrates 7 grams; Fiber 2 grams; Fat 26 grams.

Marinade

1 cup soy sauce

2 cups fresh orange juice or
   apple cider

3 cloves garlic

2 jalapeño chiles, halved

1 knob fresh ginger, peeled
   and crushed

½ bunch cilantro, stemmed
   and coarsely chopped

¼ cup maple syrup

6 8-ounce salmon fillets

olive oil

Garnishes

Papaya Salsa (p. 36)

Cilantro Cream (p. 22)

GRILL-SMOKED SALMON

SERVES 6

I have prepared this for many food events and it has always been well received. The recipe is for fillets; however, you could do a side of salmon for a buffet using the same method. I have given several cooking methods: plank cooking is a good choice if you do not have a smoker to pre-smoke the fish as it gives a slight smoky flavor. Plank cooking is excellent for many kinds of fish, poultry, beef, or pork. Fish stays moist and captures subtle wood flavor.

Ask the butcher to remove the skin, if possible.

Combine the soy sauce, orange juice or cider, garlic, chiles, ginger, cilantro, and maple syrup and place in a resealable bag. Marinate the salmon fillets for 6 hours—no longer. Remove and discard the marinade.

Prepare a smoker and smoke the salmon for 5 minutes. Do not smoke longer. Clean grill and then rub vigorously with vegetable oil. Preheat the grill on high.

To grill: Brush the salmon lightly with olive oil and place skin side down on a pre-heated grill. Grill on high heat, covered, for 5 minutes, turn the fish over and grill an additional 12 to 15 minutes, uncovered. If the butcher hasn't already done so, remove skin and transfer the salmon to serving plates. Cooking time will vary depending on the heat of the grill and the thickness of the fish. To be sure salmon is fully cooked (but not overcooked), you can grill the fish for 5 minutes (after turning), covered, then turn off the grill and leave the fish covered for 12 to 20 minutes.

To oven cook on a plank: Choose alderwood for best results. Before baking, rub the plank with cooking oil to season the wood. This won't be necessary after 8 to 10 times. Put the plank in a cold oven, mid to upper rack. Set oven on 350° (bake). When oven reaches 350°, lightly brush the salmon with olive oil and place on the plank. Bake for 20 to 25 minutes, or until fully cooked. Convection ovens will take less time.

To cook on a plank with a grill or to grill with a plank: You can use a plank on your grill, but it is necessary to soak the plank first for at least one hour. You *must* grill on indirect heat. Preheat the grill on one side to high. Grill the plank over high heat for about 6 to 8 minutes, or until lightly charred. Turn the plank over and place on the unheated side of the grill. Brush the plank with oil and place the salmon on the plank skin side down. Grill, covered, for about 25 to 30 minutes. The plank cannot be reused as often as with the oven method.

NUTRITIONAL ANALYSIS (PER SALMON FILLET, WITHOUT GARNISHES)

Calories 539 (50% from fat); Protein 65 grams;
Carbohydrates less than 1 gram; Fiber less than 1 gram;
Fat 30 grams.

3 tablespoons BBQ spice
   mix

¼ teaspoon cayenne pepper

½ teaspoon salt

1 teaspoon onion powder

1 package sugar substitute

6 7–8-ounce salmon fillets

juice from one lime

2 tablespoons maple syrup

Grilled Corn and Pepper
   Salsa (p. 29)

1 tablespoon olive oil

Garnish

Cilantro Cream (p. 22).

Green Chile Spoon Bread
   (p. 181)

BARBECUED SALMON WITH CILANTRO CREAM

SERVES 6

The barbecue seasoning gives the salmon a slightly spicy flavor. Serve it on warm Grilled Corn and Pepper Salsa or Corn and Green Chile Spoon Bread and drizzle with Cilantro Cream. This same seasoning is also suitable for catfish, redfish, or flounder.

Preheat oven to 400°.

To prepare seasoning mix, combine BBQ spice, cayenne pepper, salt, onion powder, and sugar substitute in a small bowl.

Put salmon fillets on a large plate. Pour fresh lime juice over them and let stand about 10 minutes.

Brush maple syrup over the fillets and then sprinkle seasoning mix evenly over the top. Place salmon on a cookie sheet and bake 5 minutes. Remove salmon from the oven, lightly spray the top of the salmon with an olive-oil cooking spray, and resume baking for an additional 12 to 15 minutes.

If using Grilled Corn and Pepper Salsa, add 1 tablespoon olive oil and heat to warm. Serve the salmon on warm Grilled Corn and Pepper Salsa or Corn and Green Chile Spoon Bread, drizzled with Cilantro Cream.

**NUTRITIONAL ANALYSIS
(PER SERVING, WITHOUT GARNISHES)**

Calories 500 (47% from fat); Protein 60 grams;
Carbohydrates 7 grams; Fiber 1 gram; Fat 26 grams.

PECAN CRUSTED
SEA BASS

SERVES 4

This is a good way to cook sea bass or any moderately thick white fish with a flaky texture. You can serve the fish on a bed of spaghetti squash with Roasted Red Bell Pepper Sauce for a colorful, delicious entrée that looks and tastes anything but low-fat or low-carb. The spaghetti squash is a good substitute for white starches.

Preheat the oven to 350°.

Combine the chicken broth and light butter. Microwave on high 5 seconds to melt butter and set aside.

Put the Margarita mix in a resealable bag. Add filets and seal. Marinate, refrigerated, for 15 minutes.

Using a food processor fitted with the metal blade, pulse to chop nuts with parsley or cilantro. Transfer to a shallow plate.

Preheat the oven to 375°. Remove the filets from the marinade. Brush them with olive oil and season with salt and pepper. Coat the top of the filets with the pecan mixture. Transfer to a cookie sheet, with sides, that has been sprayed with an olive-oil cooking spray. Bake for 6 minutes, then spoon the remaining chicken broth mixture over the top of each filet. Bake an additional 8 to 10 minutes, using the lesser time for 1-inch filets.

SPAGHETTI SQUASH

This is a most versatile vegetable. Spaghetti squash can be prepared in advance and reheated in an oven or microwave. You can toss it with julienned zucchini and serve with Tomato Sauce. You can top spaghetti squash with toasted pecans or sliced almonds, or grated Parmesan cheese.

To prepare the squash, pierce the skin with the tines of a fork and place on foil on a cookie sheet. Bake 45 to 60 minutes (depending on the size of the squash) or until soft when tested with

¾ cup chicken broth

2 tablespoons light butter

1 medium spaghetti squash

salt and pepper

½ cup snipped chives or
    green part of scallions,
    cut into 1½-inch lengths

3 cups Margarita mix

4 8-ounce sea bass fillets,
    1–1½ inches thick

¾ cup pecan halves

1 cup fresh parsley or
    cilantro leaves, packed

olive oil

salt and pepper

Sauce

Roasted Red Bell Pepper
    Sauce (p. 127)

(continued)

a fork. If you overcook the squash, the strands will be softer, rather than al dente, but the taste will be the same. Cool about 5 minutes, then cut in half and remove the seeds. Using a fork, scoop out the pulp into a bowl. It will come out in strands, like spaghetti. Toss with salt, pepper, chives or scallions, and 2 to 3 tablespoons of the chicken broth mixture. Cover and keep warm in a 180° oven or warming drawer until ready.

Arrange the squash in the center of 4 serving plates. Put the sea bass on top. Spoon the Roasted Red Bell Pepper Sauce around the plate.

**NUTRITIONAL ANALYSIS
(PER SERVING, WITHOUT SAUCE)**

Calories 561 (46% from fat); Protein 61 grams;
Carbohydrates 14 grams; Fiber 3 grams; Fat 29 grams.

SAUTEED SOLE WITH QUESO AND SPINACH

SERVES 4

Use only fresh fish for this dish as frozen fish, particularly if thin, tends to be watery. Flounder or tilapia may also be used. This is a good menu for a small dinner party—particularly when you know your guests are watching their carb intake.

Prepare the Queso and set aside. Put thawed spinach in a colander and press firmly to remove all the moisture.

Meanwhile, spray a medium-sized sauce pan withan olive-oil cooking spray. Add onion and bell pepper and sauté a few minutes to soften. Add spinach and stir to combine ingredients and heat thoroughly. Season with salt and pepper.

Spray a large sauce pan with an olive-oil cooking spray and place over medium heat. Add olive oil and butter. Heat until the butter sizzles.

Cut the fillets into 8 pieces, approximately the same size. Season with salt and pepper and sauté fillets on both sides for a total of about 5 minutes.

Using heat-proof entrée plates, divide spinach between 4 plates. Arrange 2 pieces of the sole on each plate, with one fillet atop the other. Spoon Queso over the top, and place in a 375° oven to heat thoroughly, about 5 minutes.

Serve immediately, with additional warm Queso on the side.

1 16-ounce bag frozen
   chopped spinach, thawed
½ onion, chopped
½ red bell pepper, chopped
salt and pepper

1 tablespoon olive oil
2 tablespoons light butter
2 pounds fresh sole fillets
salt and pepper

Sauce
8 tablespoons Queso (p. 41)

NUTRITIONAL ANALYSIS (PER SERVING)
Calories 394 (32% from fat); Protein 59 grams;
Carbohydrates 8 grams; Fiber 1 gram; Fat 14 grams.

---

6 whole eggs

1 cup low-fat cottage cheese

¾ cup grated Manchego cheese

1 cup grated Havarti or Muenster cheese

½ cup diced onion

¼ cup diced red bell pepper

3–4 sprigs fresh parsley

2 teaspoons baking powder

3 tablespoons flour

pinch cayenne pepper

1 cup fresh lump crabmeat

12 fresh shrimp peeled and deveined (21–25 count)

1 tablespoon light butter

1 tablespoon snipped chives

salt and pepper

Sauce

Roasted Red Bell Pepper Sauce (p. 127) or Quick Winter Salsa (p. 32)

Note: If using shrimp or lobster in place of the crab, use the same amount as the crab, chopped coarsely.

If you do not have a food processor, use a blender to blend the cottage cheese with 2 eggs, then transfer to a mixing bowl and add the rest of the ingredients. Finish with a hand mixer.

SHELLFISH SOUFFLES
SERVES 6

This light brunch or luncheon dish has the texture of a quiche without the crust. You can use almost any shellfish or combination of shellfish. While this is made with fresh lump crabmeat, garnishing with whole shrimp is visually appealing.

Either Roasted Red Bell Pepper Sauce or Quick Winter Salsa complements the shellfish.

Preheat the oven to 350°.

Prepare the sauce of choice and set aside.

Coat 6 8-ounce custard cups with a vegetable-oil cooking spray and set aside.

Using a food processor fitted with the metal blade, process the eggs, cottage cheese, and grated cheeses about a minute, or until well combined. Add onion, red bell pepper, and parsley, and process briefly.

Combine the baking powder with flour and cayenne pepper. Add flour mixture and crabmeat to the egg and cheese mixture and pulse several times to combine.

Pour the mixture into the custard cups and bake 20 minutes, or until soft set, puffed and lightly browned. Cool a few minutes before unmolding.

Place a medium skillet over medium-high heat. Spray with an olive-oil cooking spray and add butter. Sauté shrimp, turning at least once, until they turn pink. Season with chives, and salt and pepper. This takes just a few minutes.

To serve, first run a knife around the edge of each custard cup. Place a plate on top and turn over quickly to unmold. Surround each soufflé with sauce, and top with two of the cooked shrimp.

**NUTRITIONAL ANALYSIS
(PER SERVING, WITHOUT SAUCES)**

Calories 358 (53% from fat); Protein 36 grams;
Carbohydrates 7 grams; Fiber less than 1 gram; Fat 21 grams.

TEQUILA SHRIMP

SERVES 6

This is a fun and easy way to cook shrimp. You can serve it over Cornmeal Pudding or Wild Pecan Rice. This is a light meal, so plan to serve some appetizers and a salad.

Prepare the Cornmeal Pudding or Wild Pecan Rice and set aside.

Heat the oil and butter in a large skillet over medium-high heat. Add shrimp, garlic, shallots, and peppers and sauté, turning often, about 2 minutes. Add tequila, lime juice, and orange juice and let simmer until shrimp are pink, firm, and opaque in the center. Add salt and pepper and parsley. Remove from the heat.

Divide the Cornmeal Pudding or Wild Pecan Rice between serving plates. Remove shrimp with a slotted spoon and place over the pudding. Return the skillet to medium heat, bring back to a simmer, and whisk in the tomatoes and butter. Spoon sauce over the shrimp.

1 tablespoon light butter

2 tablespoons olive oil

36 large fresh shrimp, peeled and deveined (21–25 count)

2 cloves garlic, minced

2 shallots, minced

½ red bell pepper, diced

½ yellow bell pepper, diced

⅓ cup tequila

⅓ cup fresh lime juice

⅓ cup fresh orange juice

salt and pepper

2 tablespoons minced fresh parsley

1 cup diced tomatoes

1½ tablespoons light butter

Accompaniments

Cornmeal Pudding (p. 180)

Wild Pecan Rice (p. 178)

NUTRITIONAL ANALYSIS (PER SERVING, WITHOUT ACCOMPANIMENTS)

Calories 150 (60% from fat); Protein 8 grams; Carbohydrates 7 grams; Fiber less than 1 gram; Fat 10 grams.

Marinade

3 cloves garlic, minced

½ cup fresh lime juice

½ cup tequila

2 tablespoons sugar

1 teaspoon coarse salt

1 cup safflower or olive oil

½ tablespoon coarsely
   ground black pepper

1 teaspoon crushed chile
   flakes

Chicken

4 large chicken breast
   halves, wing tip attached

salt and pepper

2–3 tablespoons minced
   fresh parsley

½ cup chicken broth

Accompaniments

Black Bean Sauce (p. 125)

½ recipe Corn and Green
   Chile Spoon Bread
   (p. 181)

Pico de Gallo (p. 28) or
   Mango Salsa (p. 35)

fresh cilantro sprigs

CHICKEN MARGARITA
SERVES 4

The chicken preparation is a little trouble but makes an attractive presentation for a special occasion. If you prefer, you can use grilled chicken breasts. Either way, this is a fun and flavorful Southwest dinner.

Advance Preparation: The marinade, Black Bean Sauce, and Pico de Gallo or Mango Salsa may be made 1 day in advance.

Preheat the oven to 400°.

Combine the garlic, lime juice, tequila, sugar, salt, safflower or olive oil, pepper, and chile flakes and place in a 7 × 11 glass dish.

Remove skin and visible fat from the chicken breasts. Using a sharp knife, remove the breast bones and cut the joint at the wing to release the wing. Clip the wing end, leaving only the meatier joint. Trim away the skin and flesh from the end of the wing. Place chicken breasts in the marinade, cover, and refrigerate 2 hours.

Remove the chicken from the marinade. Take the narrow end of the breast and pull it around to the base of the wing joint. Secure with a toothpick. Place the breasts in a baking dish just large enough to accommodate all four breasts.

Season with salt and pepper. Using a pastry brush, brush the chicken with the marinade and sprinkle with minced parsley. Pour ½ cup of the marinade in the pan along with the chicken broth.

Bake the chicken on the middle rack, at 400°, 15 minutes. Turn the setting to broil for about 5 minutes, until the top is lightly browned.

Pool half of each serving plate with Black Bean Sauce. Remove toothpicks and place the chicken on the sauce. Serve the Corn and Green Chile Spoon Bread in a tamale husk and garnish the plates with Pico de Gallo or Mango Salsa, and fresh cilantro.

NUTRITIONAL ANALYSIS (PER SERVING, WITHOUT ACCOMPANIMENTS)

Calories 359 (32% from fat); Protein 54 grams;
Carbohydrates 1 gram; Fiber less than 1 gram; Fat 13 grams.

BLACK BEAN SAUCE

MAKES 4 CUPS

Heat a 2-quart saucepan over medium heat. Coat with a vegetable-oil cooking spray and add garlic and shallots. Stirring constantly, sauté 1 to 2 minutes, then add white wine, sherry, black beans, and 1½ cups chicken broth. Bring to a simmer and cook 6 to 8 minutes, stirring frequently. Transfer the beans to a blender or food processor fitted with the metal blade and blend until very smooth.

Pour the puréed beans back into the same pan over medium-low heat. Add chili powder and enough additional chicken broth to make a sauce the consistency of heavy cream. Season with cilantro, salt, and pepper.

1 tablespoon minced garlic

2 tablespoon minced shallots

¼ cup white wine

⅛ cup sherry

1½ cups cooked black beans

2–3 cups chicken broth

1 teaspoon chili powder

1 tablespoon minced cilantro

salt and pepper

NUTRITIONAL ANALYSIS (PER ½ CUP)
Calories 56 (6% from fat); Protein 3 grams;
Carbohydrates 9 grams; Fiber 3 grams; Fat less than 1 gram.

1½ cups cornbread crumbs
(about 8 mini muffins)

2 tablespoons finely
chopped pecans

¼ teaspoon cayenne pepper

2 tablespoons fresh minced
parsley

5 large skinless boneless
chicken breasts halves

salt and pepper

3 tablespoons light butter

1½ cups chicken broth,
divided use

½ cup white wine

juice from ½ lemon

Sauce

Roasted Red Bell Pepper
Sauce (p. 127)

sprigs of fresh parsley

CORNBREAD CRUSTED CHICKEN

SERVES 5

This is a good way to bake skinless chicken breasts to preserve the natural juices. Try the same recipe for fish fillets such as catfish, halibut, or red snapper as both the cornbread crust and Roasted Red Bell Pepper Sauce will complement fish as well as chicken.

Preheat the oven to broil. Place the rack in the middle of the oven.

Combine the cornbread crumbs with pecans. Sprinkle cayenne pepper and parsley over the top and toss with two forks to disperse seasoning evenly.

Coat a baking dish with a vegetable-oil cooking spray. Season chicken with salt and pepper on both sides and place in the dish. Put about 1½ tablespoons of the cornbread topping on each one. Melt the butter in ½ cup chicken broth and moisten the crumb topping with about 2 teaspoons liquid. Position the rack in the center of the oven. Broil for 8 minutes or until lightly browned. Change the oven setting to bake and set the temperature at 350°. Pour the remaining broth, wine, and lemon juice in the baking pan and bake an additional 8 to 10 minutes.

To serve, pool the plate with the Roasted Red Bell Pepper Sauce and serve one breast per person. Garnish with sprigs of fresh parsley.

NUTRITIONAL ANALYSIS
(PER SERVING, WITHOUT SAUCE)

Calories 454 (36% from fat); Protein 65 grams;
Carbohydrates 8 grams; Fiber less than 1 gram; Fat 18 grams.

ROASTED RED BELL PEPPER SAUCE

To make the sauce, cut the peppers in small pieces and place in a blender. Turn the blender on/off to chop. Coat a small skillet with a vegetable-oil cooking spray and sauté the garlic and shallots a few minutes to soften, then add white wine and lemon juice. Blend with peppers until smooth. Add chicken broth and cornstarch and blend again.

Transfer mixture to a small saucepan and cook over medium heat until thickened, about 2 to 3 minutes. Stir in cream cheese and tomato paste. Season to taste with salt and pepper. If the sauce is not smooth, blend again.

2 large red bell peppers, roasted and peeled

2 cloves garlic, minced

2 shallots, minced

¼ cup white wine

juice from 1 lemon

½ cup chicken broth

1 tablespoon cornstarch

1½ ounces light or low-fat cream cheese

1 tablespoon tomato paste

salt and pepper

NUTRITIONAL ANALYSIS (PER ½ CUP, BASED ON 4 CUPS PER RECIPE)

Calories 36 (37% from fat); Protein 1 grams;
Carbohydrates 5 grams; Fiber less than 1 gram; Fat 1.5 grams.

¼ cup almonds

1 large shallot

¾ cup Montreal chicken
    seasoning

1 tablespoon lemon pepper

1 cup fresh parsley leaves,
    packed

⅔ cup chicken broth

1 tablespoon light butter

5 large chicken breasts, on
    the bone

5 thin slices Oaxaca,
    Manchego, or smoked
    Gouda cheese

OAXACA STUFFED CHICKEN BREASTS

SERVES 5

Whether grilled or roasted, chicken cooked on the bone produces juicier, tenderer meat than boneless chicken. The seasoning mix replaces the skin which helps seal in the juices. Basting the chicken with some chicken broth creates some flavorful natural juices. Serve the chicken with your favorite vegetables for a meal low in calories, carbs, and fats.

Preheat oven to 350°.

Using a food processor fitted with the metal blade, process the almonds, shallot, seasoning mix, lemon pepper, and parsley to make coarse crumbs. Set aside.

Combine chicken broth and butter. Microwave on high for 5 seconds to melt butter.

Remove the skin and visible fat from the chicken. Trim away excess boney area next to the thin edge of the breast.

Make a slit in the thickest portion of the breast, deep enough to accept the cheese and insert a slice of the cheese. Pull breast together to enclose the cheese.

Press seasoning mix on top of each chicken breast and arrange in a roasting pan that has been sprayed with a vegetable-oil cooking spray.

Bake 15 minutes, uncovered. Remove and pour chicken broth mixture evenly over all the chicken breasts. Cover and continue baking an additional 25 to 30 minutes.

Serve the chicken with your favorite accompaniment and drizzle with the pan juices.

NUTRITIONAL ANALYSIS (PER SERVING)
Calories 505 (25% from fat); Protein 73 grams;
Carbohydrates 6 grams; Fiber 3 grams; Fat 21 grams.

CHICKEN-STUFFED CHILES

SERVES 6

low-fat, low-carb

This is one of my favorite combinations of flavors. Try serving the chiles with both the Yellow Bell Pepper Sauce and the Roasted Red Bell Pepper Sauce for a colorful presentation. If you don't want to go to the trouble of preparing both sauces, serve the chiles with a mild tomato salsa.

Advance Preparation: Sauces and chiles may be prepared a day in advance.

Cook the chicken as directed (in "Basics" [p. 11]) and shred or cut the meat into small pieces into a large bowl. Season with salt and pepper.

Coat a medium skillet with a vegetable-oil cooking spray and sauté shallots and garlic over medium heat until softened. Add chicken broth, goat or ricotta cheese, and cream cheese and remove from heat. Stir to combine the cheeses. Season with salt and pepper. Fold cheese mixture into the chicken.

Using scissors, make a slit on the side of each chile and remove seeds and veins carefully. Stuff each chile with the chicken and cheese mixture. Coat an 8-inch or 9-inch round pie pan with a vegetable-oil cooking spray and place chiles in a circle, stems overlapping the edge of the dish.

Preheat the oven to 375°.

Combine the cornbread crumbs with pecans and cilantro. Melt the butter in the chicken broth.

Top each chile with 1 to 2 tablespoons of the cornbread crumbs. Moisten the crumbs with butter and chicken broth. Put remaining crumbs on a cookie sheet and moisten with broth. Cover the chiles with foil and bake for 8 minutes. Uncover and bake 12 to 15 minutes or until heated through and the crumbs are lightly browned. Toast the additional crumbs on the baking sheet at the same time until lightly browned.

4 chicken breasts, roasted

salt and pepper

2 shallots, minced

1 clove garlic, minced

2–3 tablespoons chicken broth

2 ounces low-fat goat cheese or low-fat ricotta cheese

2 ounces light or low-fat cream cheese

salt and pepper

6 large poblano chiles, roasted and peeled (stems intact)

1 cup cornbread crumbs (about 6 miniature muffins)

3 tablespoons chopped pecans

1 tablespoon minced cilantro

2 tablespoons light butter, melted

¼ cup chicken broth

Sauces

Yellow Bell Pepper Sauce (p. 112)

Roasted Red Bell Pepper Sauce (p. 127)

Garnish

fresh cilantro sprigs

(continued)

For individual servings, pool each plate with the Yellow Bell Pepper Sauce and the Roasted Red Bell Pepper Sauce and serve one chile per person. Sprinkle some of the toasted additional crumbs on the plate and garnish with fresh cilantro sprigs.

OTHER SUGGESTED FILLINGS AND SAUCES

1. Substitute shrimp for the chicken, add fresh corn kernels, and serve with Roasted Red Bell Pepper Sauce.

2. Fill chiles with Picadillo (p. 138) and serve with a mild tomato sauce.

NUTRITIONAL ANALYSIS
(PER SERVING, WITHOUT SAUCE)

Calories 330 (35% from fat); Protein 41 grams;
Carbohydrates 12 grams; Fiber 1 gram; Fat 13 grams.

VEAL CHOPS WITH MUSHROOMS AND MANCHEGO SAUCE

SERVES 4

Sauce

1 poblano chile, roasted and peeled

1 clove garlic, minced

1 shallot, minced

1½ cups water, divided use

1 package Au Jus Gravy mix

2 ounces Manchego cheese, grated

salt and pepper to taste

4 veal chops, at least 1½ inches thick

olive oil

Montreal steak seasoning

10 whole mushrooms, stemmed and sliced

Accompaniment

Oven-Roasted Onions (p. 173)

Corn and Green Chile Spoon Bread (p. 181)

Chipotle Mashed Sweet Potatoes (p. 176)

Veal chops are not inexpensive but do make a memorable meal. Order them with the bone "on the bottom" (the butcher will understand) so all the meat is on one side of the bone, rather than the bone being through the middle of the chop. Serve with the Oven-Roasted Onions and fresh asparagus. The Manchego Sauce is quick and simple to make. Grilling the chops briefly and then finishing them in the oven gives the cook a little time to assemble the rest of the meal. Suggested accompaniments are Corn and Green Chile Spoon Bread or Chipotle Mashed Sweet Potatoes.

This sauce is equally good on tenderloin steaks or slices of a whole tenderloin.

Preheat the oven to 300°.

To make the sauce, first cut the roasted poblano chile into thin strips. Set aside.

Spray a small saucepan with a vegetable coating spray and place over medium heat. Add garlic and shallots and sauté until lightly browned. (Add additional spray if necessary.) Add ¾ cups of the water and simmer 5 to 6 minutes. Strain, reserving the liquid.

Return liquid to the same saucepan adding remaining ¾ cups water and contents of the Au Jus Gravy mix. Stir constantly over medium heat until thickened. Add the cheese, stirring until melted. Add poblano chile strips and remove from heat. (The mushrooms will be cooked and added last.)

Trim as much fat from the veal chops as possible. Brush with olive oil on both sides, and season with steak seasoning. Preheat an outdoor grill on high heat.

Place chops in the middle of the grill. Grill, covered, about 5 minutes to mark the "presentation" side. Transfer to the oven to finish cooking for 20 to 25 minutes.

(continued)

Meanwhile, using a medium-sized skillet which has been coated with an olive-oil cooking spray, sauté the mushroom slices a few minutes or until lightly browned. Remove and place on a paper towel, then place in the roasting pan with the veal chops to keep warm.

To serve, place a veal chop on each serving plate topped with mushrooms. Spoon the Manchego Sauce over the top.

Serve with Corn and Green Chile Spoon Bread, Chipotle Mashed Sweet Potatoes, or, for fewer carbs, Oven-Roasted Onions and fresh asparagus.

NUTRITIONAL ANALYSIS (PER SERVING, WITHOUT ACCOMPANIMENTS)

Calories 384 (56% from fat); Protein 42 grams; Carbohydrates less than 1 gram; Fiber less than 1 gram; Fat 24 grams.

NUTRITIONAL ANALYSIS (MANCHEGO SAUCE, PER SERVING, BASED ON FOUR SERVINGS)

Calories 70 (51% from fat); Protein 5 grams; Carbohydrates 4 grams; Fiber less than 1 gram; Fat 4 grams.

GRILLED PORK TENDERLOIN WITH RASPBERRY CHIPOTLE SAUCE

SERVES 8

The brine makes the tenderloins very moist and juicy, even if you cook them well done. You can buy the raspberry chipotle sauce at most supermarkets. It is the condiment many people serve on a block of cream cheese for an appetizer, but it also makes a gravy mix something special.

Brining pork chops or wild game will produce a tender and juicy result.

To make the sauce, place a small saucepan over medium-high heat. Add shallot, vinegar, and ¾ cups water, and bring to a boil. Reduce heat and simmer until shallot is very tender. Add the raspberry chipotle sauce and stir to combine. Remove and strain the mixture to remove most of the seeds. Put the strained mixture back in the same saucepan, and stir in remaining water and Au Jus Gravy mix. Stir constantly over medium heat until thickened. Stir in butter and set aside.

In a large saucepan, over high heat, bring cider, water, and salt to a boil. Cool completely. Add jalapeño chiles and pour into an oversized resealable bag. Add the pork, seal, place in a large bowl, and refrigerate at least 12 hours or up to 18 hours.

Preheat oven to 350°.

When ready to grill the meat, preheat an outdoor grill to the highest setting. Remove the pork from the brine and discard the brine.

Pat the tenderloins dry and then rub with olive oil. Season on all sides with steak seasoning. Grill 6 minutes per side, covered, turning once or twice to sear all sides.

Transfer to a baking sheet and continue to cook in the oven for 25 minutes. After 15 minutes, reduce the heat to 275°.

Raspberry Chipotle Sauce

1 large shallot

2 tablespoons balsamic vinegar

1½ cups water

⅓ cup raspberry chipotle sauce

1 package Au Jus Gravy mix

1 tablespoon light butter

Brine

1 cup apple cider

4 cups water

3 tablespoons coarse salt (not ground)

3 jalapeño chiles, chopped

2 pork tenderloins, about 1½ pounds each

olive oil

Montreal steak seasoning

Accompaniments

Oven-Roasted Onions (p. 173)

Wild Pecan Rice (p. 178) or Chipotle Mashed Sweet Potatoes (p. 176)

(continued)

Transfer the pork to a cutting board and cover with foil while you reheat the sauce.

Slice the pork and drizzle with some of the sauce. Serve with Oven-Roasted Onions and Wild Pecan Rice, or Chipotle Mashed Sweet Potatoes.

NUTRITIONAL ANALYSIS (PER SERVING, WITHOUT ACCOMPANIMENTS)

Calories 331 (39% from fat); Protein 48 grams;
Carbohydrates 1 gram; Fiber less than 1 gram; Fat 14.5 grams.

NUTRITIONAL ANALYSIS (RASPBERRY CHIPOTLE SAUCE, PER SERVING, BASED ON 8 SERVINGS)

Calories 39 (23% from fat); Protein less than 1 gram;
Carbohydrates 7 grams; Fiber less than 1 gram; Fat 1 gram.

BRAISED PORK TENDERLOIN WITH CHIPOTLE WHISKEY SAUCE

SERVES 8

A good dish for entertaining, the sauce can be prepared in advance and reheated. While it has a lot of ingredients, it is not hard to make and well worth the effort. You will like it also on steaks or veal chops. Cornmeal Pudding and a simple vegetable can be made while the pork is cooking. For a lower carb meal, serve a colorful assortment of vegetables in place of the Cornmeal Pudding.

Preheat oven to 325°.

Combine the bourbon, maple syrup, soy sauce, and cider in an oversized resealable bag.

Trim excess fat from the tenderloins and place in the marinade for at least 5 hours or overnight. When ready to cook, remove from marinade and discard the marinade.

Place a roasting pan that is large enough to accommodate both tenderloins over medium high heat. Add just enough olive oil to lightly coat the pan. Season the pork with salt and pepper and sear, turning to brown all sides, about 3 to 4 minutes.

Place roasting pan in the preheated oven and roast for 30 minutes, or until the internal temperature registers 135°. Remove pork and cover tightly with foil. Let stand about 5 minutes. (The meat will continue to cook.)

When ready to serve, reheat the sauce, stirring constantly. Slice the pork and arrange slices on each serving plate. Drizzle with the sauce, serving additional sauce on the side. Serve with Cornmeal Pudding.

⅔ cup bourbon

½ cup low-calorie maple syrup

½ cup soy sauce

1 cup apple cider

2 pork tenderloins (not marinated)

olive oil

salt and pepper

Accompaniment
Cornmeal Pudding (p. 180)

NUTRITIONAL ANALYSIS (PER SERVING, WITHOUT SAUCE OR GARNISH)
Calories 339 (38% from fat); Protein 48 grams;
Carbohydrates 4 grams; Fiber less than 1 gram; Fat 14.5 grams.

2 shallots, chopped

4 tomatillos, husked, cored, and quartered

2½ cups water, divided use

⅓ cup whiskey (such as Jack Daniels)

⅛ cup low-calorie maple syrup

2 teaspoons chipotle chiles, including adobo sauce

2 tablespoons soy sauce

2 packages Au Jus Gravy mix

2 tablespoons light butter

CHIPOTLE WHISKEY SAUCE

MAKES ABOUT 2½ CUPS

Coat a medium saucepan with a vegetable-oil cooking spray. Add shallots and tomatillos and sauté until tomatillos are softened. Add 1 cup water and whiskey and simmer 4 to 5 minutes. Strain liquid to remove small seeds from the tomatillos. Return the strained liquid to the same saucepan and add maple syrup, chipotle, and soy sauce and cook another 5 minutes. Remove and cool. Transfer to a blender jar and blend until smooth.

Stir together remaining water and au jus gravy mix. Combine with blended mixture in the same saucepan. Bring to a boil, stirring constantly. Stir in butter and set aside until ready to serve.

NUTRITIONAL ANALYSIS (PER ⅓ CUP)

Calories 63 (43% from fat); Protein 2 gram;
Carbohydrates 7 grams; Fiber less than 1 gram; Fat 3 grams.

STUFFED CHILES POBLANO

SERVES 6

The fillings and sauces for these flavorful chiles are limited only by your imagination. Poblano chiles are hotter than Anaheim chiles, so choose a filling that is mild.

Preheat oven to 375°.

Roast and peel the chiles, being careful not to tear the flesh. Use scissors to make a slit down the center and to cut away the seeds and membrane. Fill each chile with about ¾ cup Picadillo and place in an 8-inch or 9-inch pie pan, with the stems towards the edge of the dish. Cover with foil and heat in a 375° oven for 10 to 15 minutes.

To make the sauce, purée the tomatoes in a blender or food processor fitted with the metal blade. Heat the oil in a medium skillet over medium heat and sauté onion and garlic until translucent, about 3 to 4 minutes. Add tomatoes and simmer 3 to 4 minutes stirring constantly. Season with fresh cilantro or basil, salt, and pepper.

Combine the sour cream and chicken broth. Season with salt and pepper. Place a dollop of cream on top of each baked chile. Pool each plate with tomato sauce and garnish with toasted almonds or pumpkin seeds.

6 large poblano chiles, roasted and peeled

Picadillo (p. 138)

Tomato Sauce

1 14½-ounce can tomatoes, including juices

1–2 teaspoons safflower oil

3 tablespoons minced onion

1 clove garlic, finely minced

1 tablespoon minced fresh cilantro or basil

salt and pepper

1 cup light sour cream

¼ cup chicken broth

salt and pepper

Garnish

⅔ cup sliced almonds or pumpkin seeds, toasted

NUTRITIONAL ANALYSIS (PER SERVING)
Calories 365 (42% from fat); Protein 20 grams;
Carbohydrates 33 grams; Fiber 6 grams; Fat 17 grams.

1¼ pounds ground turkey

1 cup chopped onion

2 teaspoons chili powder

½ teaspoon ground cumin

1 small apple, diced

1 4½-ounce can diced green
chiles

1 cup peeled and diced
sweet potato

½ 14½-ounce can Mexican-
style diced tomatoes,
tomatoes chopped

½ cup beef broth

1 tablespoon apple cider
vinegar

½ teaspoon ground
cinnamon

¼ teaspoon ground cloves

¼ cup seedless raisins or
dried cranberries

1 teaspoon salt

Pinch white pepper

PICADILLO

MAKES 6 CUPS

Picadillo is a delicious filling for soft tacos, lettuce wraps, or spicy poblano chiles. While not exactly low-fat, duck is excellent in this recipe. For hunters of wild game, venison is a good choice, if ground without added fat.

Heat a large skillet over medium heat. Add the turkey and sear, without stirring, until browned. (Don't be concerned about the brown bits in the pan.) When well browned, add the onion, chili powder, and cumin and mix in well, breaking up clumps of meat with a fork. Stir in the apple, chiles, sweet potato, tomatoes, and beef broth. Simmer, covered 15 minutes.

Stir in the vinegar, cinnamon, cloves or dried cranberries, raisins, salt, and white pepper and cook uncovered about 10 to 15 minutes or until vegetables are tender and most of the liquid has been absorbed. Adjust seasonings to taste.

> **NUTRITIONAL ANALYSIS**
> **(PER 1 CUP PICADILLO ONLY,**
> **BASED ON 6 CUPS PER RECIPE)**
> Calories 237 (30% from fat); Protein 17 grams;
> Carbohydrates 24 grams; Fiber 3 grams; Fat 8 grams.

Soft Tacos:
Put a generous spoonful of Picadillo in a softened, warm flour or corn tortilla, fold over, and serve two per person. Garnish with one of the salsas or Pico de Gallo (p. 28).

7

Tortilla Specialties

Let the quality of your ingredients speak to you. Taste things half done—and overdone. Taste everything you cook and take nothing for granted. Even your palate can change.

—James Beard

Enchiladas, chalupas, tacos—these are the heart and soul of Mexican food and an inspiration for Southwest food. "Authentic" preparations of these wonderful foods often include massive amounts of lard or bacon fat to refry beans, to soften and seal corn tortillas for enchiladas, to deep-fry tortillas for tacos, chalupas, or chips, and to tenderize flour when making flour tortillas.

In this chapter, you'll find new techniques that bypass these fat-infused methods as well as enchilada sauces that range from fat-free to low-fat. Tomatillo Sauce (p. 158), Ranchero Sauce (p. 159), and Spicy Enchilada Sauce (p. 156) rely on combinations of tomatoes, chiles, onions, fresh herbs, and spices for their zesty flavors. Fish tacos, lettuce wrap tacos, and other soft tacos are a part of contemporary Southwest cuisine.

Enchilada and taco fillings range from chicken to combinations of cheese and vegetables. Chalupa shells topped with well-seasoned beans, grilled chicken, or fresh crabmeat with crisp lettuce, ripe tomatoes, and a fresh salsa are as easy to make as they are light.

When preparing tacos, chalupas, and other tortilla specialties, always let personal taste be your guide. Freely substitute fillings, greens, or salsas. The combinations that are given are some of my "tasters'" and my favorites.

Garnishes

salsa

mixed greens

Taco Meat

1 pound ground turkey or
  ground top round

1 cup diced yellow or white
  onion

1 clove garlic, minced

1½ teaspoons chili powder

1 teaspoon dried oregano

⅔ cup tomato sauce

½ cup diced green chiles,
  undrained

½ teaspoon salt

¼ teaspoon coarsely ground
  black pepper

A no-carb alternative:
Remember, anything
served in a taco can be
served in a Lettuce Wrap
(p. 145), eliminating the
carbs in the corn tortilla
and almost all carbs in
the recipe.

TACOS

FILLS 8 TACOS

For crispy tacos, buy tacos that are lowest in fat and carbs. It is very hard to bake your own and save many carbs or fat.

For soft tacos, soften fresh corn tortillas, 3 at a time, in the microwave on high for 15 seconds.

For each taco, fill first with warm Taco Meat, Seasoned Chicken, or bite-sized pieces of cooked pork tenderloin or steak, or Picadillo (p. 138)

Add:

➡ shredded lettuce or finely shredded cabbage

➡ grated low-fat cheese or warm Queso (p. 41)

➡ diced tomatoes or Pico de Gallo (p. 28)

Serve tacos with a salsa and garnish plates with mixed greens

TACO MEAT

FILLS 8 TACOS OR 8 ENCHILADAS

When testing this recipe with ground turkey, my "tasters" all thought the filling was beef. Using onions and adding green chiles add flavor and reduce the amount of meat (and calories) in each taco.

Heat a large skillet over medium heat. Add the turkey or ground round and sear over medium heat until browned, without stirring, about 5 to 6 minutes. (If using beef, pour off all rendered fat.) Add the onion, garlic, chili powder, and oregano and stir to break up clumps of meat. Sauté until the onion is fully cooked, about 3 to 4 minutes. Lower the heat to medium low and stir in the tomato sauce and chiles.

Simmer until most of the liquid has evaporated, about 5 to 8 minutes. Add salt and pepper.

**NUTRITIONAL ANALYSIS (PER SERVING WITH
GROUND TURKEY, FILLING ONLY)**
Calories 100 (32% from fat); Protein 11 grams;
Carbohydrates 6 grams; Fiber 1 gram; Fat 4 grams.

**NUTRITIONAL ANALYSIS (PER SERVING WITH
GROUND BEEF, FILLING ONLY)**
Calories 157 (46% from fat); Protein 15 grams;
Carbohydrates 6 grams; Fiber 1 gram; Fat 8 grams.

TACO PARTY

A taco buffet is always popular for casual entertaining or a cocktail party. Guests can assemble their own tacos from a variety of fillings, sauces, salsas, and toppings. Some of the fillings are better warm, but all the accompaniments can be at room temperature.

Offer taco shells, fresh flour tortillas, and lettuce cups. Many specialty stores offer prepared salsas so your preparation can be limited to the fillings. You will need shredded lettuce, grated cheeses, Skinny Guacamole (p. 44), Pico de Gallo (p. 28), and several salsas. Choose from the many meat and chicken fillings in this book. You can add some grilled swordfish, in bite-sized pieces, for those who like fish tacos. The swordfish can be served at room temperature. You will need small appetizer plates and some napkins. Obviously this kind of buffet is not suitable for coats and ties or silk blouses. Carbs are in the tortilla shells, guacamole, and some of the fruit salsas, but when used as garnishes, they are minimal.

Suggested Fillings

Picadillo (p. 138)

Seasoned Chicken Filling (p. 12)

Cooked pork tenderloin, in cubes

Grilled salmon, flaked

Suggested Salsas

Mango Salso (p. 35)

Papaya Salsa (p. 36)

Grilled Corn and Pepper Salsa (p. 29)

Accent Sauces

Chipotle Ranch Dressing (p. 25)

Chile Poblano Cream (p. 40)

Guacamole

FISH TACOS

Fish Tacos have become very popular and can be made with fried fish, grilled fish, or pan-seared fish. You can use any firm-fleshed fish such as halibut, tuna, swordfish, mahimahi, or red snapper. Fillings can be as simple as lettuce, diced tomatoes, and cheese, or you can use any of the salsas or sauces in the Salsa section of the chapter on Basics. Whether you use soft flour or corn tortillas, or crispy taco shells, these are a fun first course or light entrée.

SUGGESTED COMBINATIONS

➡ Fried catfish, lettuce, tomatoes, and Chipotle Ranch Dressing (p. 25).

➡ Chopped shrimp, mango, watercress or sprouts, sliced scallions, and Avocado Ranch Dressing (p. 24).

➡ Grilled Swordfish, arugula, Papaya Salsa (p. 36) and Ranch Dressing.

PEPPERED TUNA TACOS

MAKES 8

The cabbage is lightly dressed so it remains crisp. This combination of ingredients is also very good with diced, cooked pork tenderloin. When I serve these, I like to offer Chipotle Ranch Dressing as an accent sauce, but they are very good with just the salsas.

Preheat the oven to 350°.

To make the slaw, combine the cabbage, scallions, and sesame seeds in a small bowl. Mix together the olive oil, vinegar, chile oil, water, salt, and lime juice. Toss cabbage mixture with 3 tablespoons of the vinaigrette.

Brush the tuna with olive oil and season on both sides with coarsely ground salt and pepper.

Grill 5 minutes per side on an outdoor grill over high heat, or pan-sear in a skillet.

To pan-sear, place a large, nonstick skillet over medium-high heat. Add a small amount of olive oil and sear the tuna, turning once, 1½ minutes per side. Transfer to the oven to finish cooking, about 6 to 7 minutes. Using a hot pad remove and cut the tuna into bite-sized pieces.

Put some of the slaw in each taco shell. Top with tuna, and Pico de Gallo or Papaya Salsa. Drizzle each taco with Chipotle Ranch.

NUTRITIONAL ANALYSIS
(PER TACO, WITHOUT SALSA)
Calories 185 (29% from fat); Protein 16 grams;
Carbohydrates 17 grams; Fiber 3 grams; Fat 6 grams.

low-fat

5 cups thinly sliced cabbage
5 scallions, trimmed and sliced
2 tablespoons toasted sesame seeds

3 tablespoons light olive oil
3 tablespoons rice wine vinegar
½ tablespoon chile oil
2 tablespoons water
¼ tablespoon salt
juice from ½ lime

1 pound fresh tuna, about 1 inch thick
olive oil
coarsely ground salt
coarsely ground black pepper

8 crisp corn tortilla shells
Pico de Gallo (p. 28) or Papaya Salsa (p. 36)

Accompaniment
Chipotle Ranch Dressing (p. 25)

Note: If preparing these as an appetizer, or if using soft corn tortillas, warm the tortillas, one at a time, in a nonstick skillet over medium heat. Gather your guests in the kitchen (they are probably there anyway) and assemble fresh, warm tacos. The tortillas will be softer and stay warm longer. Fill each tortilla with grilled tuna and let your guests add the slaw and condiments.

1 pound red snapper fillets,
   skin removed

juice from one lime

olive oil

garlic or seasoning salt and
   pepper

1 8-ounce package mixed
   baby greens

8–10 corn tortilla taco shells

3 ounces Monterrey jack or
   cheddar cheese, grated

1½ cups Pico de Gallo
   (p. 28) or Mango Salsa
   (p. 35)

Avocado Ranch Dressing
   (p. 24)

diced sweet onions
   (optional)

SEARED SNAPPER TACOS

MAKES 8–10

The Avocado Ranch dressing is a good accent sauce for these tacos and very easy to make. To ease preparation, you can buy Pico de Gallo.

To prepare the snapper, place filets on a large, shallow plate. Squeeze lime juice evenly over the fillets and let stand for 10 minutes. Discard the lime juice. Brush filets on both sides with olive oil and season with garlic or seasoning salt and pepper.

Place a large nonstick skillet over medium-high heat. Sear the snapper for 3 to 4 minutes (reduce heat to medium if necessary). Turn snapper and cook on the opposite side for 5 to 6 minutes. Fish will flake easily when fully cooked and be opaque in the center. Remove snapper and cool 5 minutes. Cut into bite-sized pieces.

Cut larger greens into smaller pieces. Put a few greens in each taco shell, then the snapper and the cheese. Top with Pico de Gallo or Mango Salsa. Arrange 2 tacos on each plate and drizzle with Avocado Ranch Dressing. Support the tacos on one end with baby greens and a ramekin of additional Avocado Ranch Dressing on the opposite end, or diced sweet onions if using.

**NUTRITIONAL ANALYSIS
(PER TACO, BASED ON EIGHT SERVINGS,
WITHOUT RANCH DRESSING OR ONIONS)**

Calories 200 (31% from fat); Protein 20 grams;
Carbohydrates 14 grams; Fiber 2 grams; Fat 7 grams.

LETTUCE WRAP TACOS

FILLS ABOUT 10 LETTUCE CUPS

Almost anything that goes into a taco can go into a lettuce cup, such as Taco Meat (p. 140), Seasoned Chicken Filling (p. 11), or Picadillo (p. 138). Prepare a couple of fillings and several salsas, and let guests fill lettuce cups with their choices. If you miss the "crunch," make some very thin tortilla strips to serve with the "tacos." The added carbs and fat will be less than using taco shells. The following filling is a favorite of mine as it has a slightly Asian flavor and is very colorful.

To prepare the lettuce cups, remove the core from iceberg lettuce. Run cold water through the core until the leaves begin to separate. Remove the lettuce from running water and gently tear away lettuce leaf cups. Dry thoroughly, then stack together and refrigerate until ready to use. If using Boston lettuce, rinse the heads under cold water and pull away leaves to separate. Boston lettuce leaves are easier to separate and offer more small cups suitable for cocktail appetizers. They are not as crisp as iceberg, however.

Prepare tortilla strips and set aside.

Put the chicken breasts in the freezer for about 45 minutes to partially freeze. This makes them much easier to dice into small pieces. Use a very sharp knife and dice the chicken. Set aside.

Dissolve chicken bouillon and cornstarch in water and set aside.

Place a large skillet or sauté pan over medium heat. Coat with an olive-oil cooking spray. Add pork or veal and chicken and sauté, breaking up the pork with a fork. Add garlic salt, mustard, scallions, and peppers and sauté a few minutes, or until chicken is just cooked. Stir in chicken bouillon mixture, oyster sauce, soy sauce, and picante sauce. Cook until sauce thickens, just a few minutes.

Serve the filling warm with lettuce cups and tortilla strips.

1 head iceberg lettuce or
  2 heads Boston leaf lettuce

thin tortilla strips (p. 9)

3 skinless boneless chicken
  breast halves

1 tablespoon dry chicken
  bouillon powder

1½ tablespoon cornstarch

⅔ cup water

¼ pound ground pork or
  veal (lean)

1½ teaspoons garlic salt

1 teaspoon dry mustard

4 scallions, trimmed and
  sliced

1 red bell pepper, roasted,
  peeled, and diced

2 poblano chiles, roasted,
  peeled, and diced

½ yellow bell pepper, diced

½ cup oyster sauce

1 tablespoon soy sauce

3 tablespoons picante sauce

NUTRITIONAL ANALYSIS (PER SERVING WITHOUT TORTILLA STRIPS)

Calories 151 (27% from fat); Protein 21 grams;
Carbohydrates 7 grams; Fiber 2 grams; Fat 4.5 grams.

low-fat

½ medium onion, thinly
   sliced

½ red bell pepper, cut into
   julienne strips

½ yellow bell pepper, cut
   into julienne strips

½ poblano chile, roasted,
   peeled, and finely diced
   or ½ cup diced green
   chiles

2 grilled chicken breast
   halves, thinly sliced

salt and pepper

6 flour tortillas or pita
   pockets, warmed

3 ounces smoked Gouda
   cheese, grated, or mild
   goat cheese, crumbled

GRILLED CHICKEN TACOS

MAKES 6

Like most tacos, these make good snacks or a light meal. Poblano chiles will make spicier tacos, green chiles milder tacos. Or, for sensitive palates, use green bell peppers. A small amount of smoked Gouda cheese gives more flavor than twice the amount of low-fat cheese.

Preheat the oven to 300°.

Place a medium skillet over medium heat and coat generously with a vegetable-oil cooking spray. Sauté the onions and bell peppers, tossing constantly, until softened. You may need additional spray to keep the peppers from burning. Add chiles and chicken and toss together. Season with salt and pepper and cook long enough to heat the chicken.

Soften the tortillas if necessary in a microwave oven or nonstick skillet (p. 152). Divide the chicken mixture between the tortillas. Top each tortilla with about ½ ounce cheese, then fold over and press down to seal.

Using a nonstick griddle or skillet, cook each tortilla quickly on both sides until lightly browned. Transfer each one to a cookie sheet and place in the oven while cooking the rest.

Serve the tacos like a sandwich, with a cup of gazpacho or a mixed green salad.

NUTRITIONAL ANALYSIS (PER TACO)

Calories 322 (28% from fat); Protein 26 grams;
Carbohydrates 32 grams; Fiber 3 grams; Fat 10 grams.

VEGGIE TACOS

MAKES 8 POCKETS

You may serve this colorful vegetable combination in pita pockets or flour tortillas. I've omitted cheese to make this dish low-fat; however, a small amount of grated cheese or Mashed Black Beans (p. 18) in each taco makes a more satisfying dish.

Bring 1 quart of salted water to a boil. Add carrot slices and cook 1 minute. Add broccoli florets and cook carrot and broccoli 1 minute together. Drain and refresh under cold water.

Halve zucchini and yellow squash lengthwise, and cut into slices.

Heat the vegetable oil in a large skillet over medium heat. Add the onion, squash, and mushrooms and season with salt and pepper. Sauté, tossing constantly, for 2 to 3 minutes. Add broccoli and carrot and cook 2 to 3 minutes or until vegetables are lightly browned and tender. Add chicken broth and soy sauce. Toss to coat and season vegetables.

Heat pita pockets or tortillas in a hot oven or microwave. Divide the vegetables between them. Fold tortillas over or roll like enchiladas. Serve 2 per person.

Garnish plates with lettuce and serve with Quick Winter Salsa and picante.

1 large carrot, thinly sliced diagonally
2 cups small broccoli florets
1 large zucchini squash
1 yellow squash
1 tablespoon vegetable oil
1 onion, thinly sliced
2 cups sliced mushrooms
salt and pepper
2–3 tablespoons chicken or beef broth
1–2 teaspoons soy sauce

8 pita pockets or 8 flour tortillas
3 cups red tip leaf lettuce, thinly sliced

Garnishes
lettuce
Quick Winter Salsa (p. 32)

NUTRITIONAL ANALYSIS
(PER PITA POCKET, WITHOUT GARNISHES)
Calories 161 (17% from fat); Protein 6 grams;
Carbohydrates 28 grams; Fiber 5 grams; Fat 3 grams.

---

6 ounces light or low-fat cream cheese

4 ounces goat cheese

2 cooked chicken breast halves

salt and pepper

3 12-inch flour tortillas

1 cup thinly sliced spinach

1 large red bell pepper, roasted, peeled, and sliced

¾ cup finely diced sweet onion

GRILLED CHICKEN TACOS WITH GOAT CHEESE AND ROASTED PEPPERS

MAKES 3 WHOLE SANDWICHES

Serve this dish like a sandwich. Many people will find that half a taco makes a meal when served with a mixed green salad or a cup of gazpacho. If you can buy smoked chicken breasts, the taste combination is delicious.

Preheat the oven to 375°.

Using a spoon, cream together the cream cheese and goat cheese. Set aside.

Shred or finely chop the chicken breasts. If dry, moisten with a little chicken broth. Season with salt and pepper.

Soften the tortillas, one at a time, in a microwave on high for 15 seconds. Working quickly, spread first with a thin layer of the cheese mixture. Top with the sliced spinach, chicken, red pepper, and onion.

Fold the edges inward about ½ inch, then tightly roll up the tortilla and place seam side down on a piece of foil. Repeat with remaining tortillas. Wrap tightly until ready to bake.

To bake, lightly coat each tortilla roll with an olive-oil cooking spray on all sides, but end with seam side down. Bake for 10 to 12 minutes, or until lightly browned. Cool about 5 minutes, then cut diagonally into two "sandwiches."

NUTRITIONAL ANALYSIS (PER ½ SANDWICH)

Calories 381 (36% from fat); Protein 29 grams; Carbohydrates 32 grams; Fiber 2 grams; Fat 15 grams.

CHICKEN CHALUPAS

MAKES 8 SERVINGS

This light luncheon dish can be prepared ahead and assembled just before serving. It is best to shred the chicken and use it while still warm or at room temperature. Serve with a cup of gazpacho.

To make the Guacamole dressing, put the chiles, tomatillos, garlic, and parsley in a blender jar and blend smooth. Add avocado, sour cream and lemon juice and blend again. Season to taste with salt and pepper. Refrigerate until ready to use.

Before cutting up the chicken, reserve all the juices in a bowl. Remove skin and cut away the meat from the chicken. Discard fat, gristle, and bones, using the white meat only. Save the dark meat for another use. Shred or cut the white meat into bite-sized pieces. Add the meat to the drippings. Stir in picante sauce. Add salt and pepper if needed.

To assemble each chalupa, place shells on 6 serving plates. Mound baby greens on the shells, then top with the seasoned chicken. Spoon the Guacamole Dressing on top and garnish with diced tomatoes and crumbled cheeses.

NUTRITIONAL ANALYSIS (PER CHALUPA WITH GUACAMOLE DRESSING)

Calories 261 (43% from fat); Protein 21 grams; Carbohydrates 16 grams; Fiber 3 gram; Fat 12.5 grams.

Guacamole Dressing

¼ cup diced green chiles

2 tomatillos, cored and quartered

1 clove garlic

5 sprigs fresh parsley

1 avocado, peeled, cored, and cut in several pieces

4 tablespoons light sour cream

1 teaspoon lemon juice

salt and white pepper to taste

1 large rotisserie chicken

4 tablespoons picante sauce

salt and pepper

8 chalupa shells

1 8-ounce package mixed baby greens (no chicory)

Garnishes

diced tomatoes

2 ounces crumbled cotija or anejo cheese

1 pound fresh crabmeat

1 cup chopped red onion

1 cup diced fresh tomatoes

½ cup diced mango or
   papaya

2 tablespoons minced fresh
   cilantro

3–4 tablespoons fresh lemon
   juice

salt and pepper

12 corn tortillas, toasted

Chile Poblano Cream
   (p. 40)

1 head romaine lettuce,
   sliced

Garnish

1 small avocado, chopped
   (optional)

CRAB CHALUPAS

MAKES 12

The combination of sweet, fresh crab and the spicy Chile Poblano
Cream makes a colorful, delicious, light chalupa.

Pick over the crabmeat and discard any bones or cartilage.

Coat a medium skillet with a vegetable-oil cooking spray
and place over medium heat. Add onion and sauté 1 to 2 minutes. Combine onion, tomatoes, mango or papaya, cilantro, and
crab in a bowl. Toss gently to combine without breaking up the
mango or papaya or crabmeat. Season with lemon juice, salt,
and pepper.

Spread each tortilla with about 2 to 3 tablespoons of Chile
Poblano Cream. Top with sliced romaine lettuce and crabmeat
mixture.

Garnish with chopped avocado if using.

**NUTRITIONAL ANALYSIS
(PER CHALUPA WITH GARNISH)**

Calories 197 (41% from fat); Protein 11 grams;
Carbohydrates 18 grams; Fiber 3 grams; Fat 9 grams.

HUEVOS RANCHEROS CASEROLE

SERVES 6

This mild breakfast casserole calls for a spicy sauce. Use either the Ranchero Sauce, Enchilada Sauce or serve it with your favorite picante sauce. The corn tortillas give a distinctive Southwest flavor but add very little fat or carbs to each serving. Like most "strata" casseroles, you can make this a day in advance. Be sure to use a food processor, as it is necessary to purée the cottage cheese.

Preheat oven to 350°.

Using a food processor fitted with the metal blade combine the eggs and egg white until well combined. Add skim milk and cottage cheese and process to combine. Stir onion and green chiles in by hand.

Coat an 8 × 8 × 2 baking dish with a vegetable-oil cooking spray. Arrange a layer of tortilla pieces in the pan (use about half). Top with half the turkey and cheese. Repeat, using the remaining tortilla pieces, turkey, and cheese. Pour egg mixture over all. Refrigerate for at least 8 hours or overnight.

Bake the casserole in the center of the oven for 35 to 40 minutes, or until the center is soft set, puffed, and lightly browned. Cut into squares and serve with Ranchero Sauce, Enchilada Sauce, or your favorite picante sauce.

5 large eggs

1 egg white

1 cup skim milk

1 cup low-fat cottage cheese

½ cup diced onion

¼ cup diced green chiles

4 corn tortillas, cut into strips or pieces

6 thin slices smoked turkey, diced

2 ounces Havarti cheese, grated

3 ounces Manchego cheese, grated

Sauces

Ranchero Sauce (p. 159), or

Enchilada Sauce (p. 155–56), or

picante sauce

NUTRITIONAL ANALYSIS
(PER SERVING, WITHOUT GARNISHES)

Calories 264 (41% from fat); Protein 25 grams; Carbohydrates 14 grams; Fiber 1 gram; Fat 12 grams.

ENCHILADAS

Enchiladas may be rolled, stacked, served in a casserole, or folded, which makes them "soft tacos." In most cases, corn tortillas are traditionally dipped in oil to soften and seal, and unfortunately, absorb quite a lot of fat. This may be the reason home cooks devised various ways to prepare casseroles with layers of fillings and tortillas, skipping this often messy procedure. Enchiladas are best when rolled and served immediately—another challenge for the cook who needs to do some advance preparation. Here are some procedures to soften the tortillas and several options for baking and reheating rolled enchiladas.

TO SOFTEN AND SEAL

Skillet Method: To soften and seal corn tortillas prior to rolling, heat a skillet, preferably nonstick, over medium heat. Using tongs to hold the tortillas, lightly coat them one at a time with a butter-flavored cooking spray, and then place in the skillet. Turn quickly, 5 or 6 times, until soft and pliable. Remove the skillet from the heat. Fill and roll the tortilla, then return the skillet to medium heat, and repeat with remaining tortillas.

Microwave Method: Microwave 2 or 3 tortillas at a time on high for 10 to 15 seconds. Cover the warmed tortillas with a lightly dampened towel while rolling and filling one at a time. This method only softens tortillas. It does not seal them. Flour tortillas do not need sealing. Soften them in a microwave oven or one at a time in a nonstick skillet over medium heat.

TO HEAT OR BAKE

To Microwave: Filled enchiladas may be wrapped in plastic wrap, 2 or 3 in a package, and reheated in a microwave oven. This method is good for preparing 3 or 4 servings. The tortillas will not dry out or fall apart (as they tend to do when covered with sauce). Microwave on high to warm, 60 to 90 seconds, and heat the sauce separately.

A microwave oven is particularly suitable for reheating enchiladas because it provides a moist heat and tortillas will not dry out. However, be very careful not to heat too long because tortillas can get quite tough.

To Prepare for Baking: Place filled enchiladas, seam side down, in a 9 × 13 baking dish. Brush the tortillas with some of the sauce and cover with plastic wrap. Press the wrap directly on the tortillas. Cover again with foil and refrigerate until ready to use. (If baking immediately, cover with foil only.)

Preheat the oven to 400°. Remove the foil and plastic wrap. Discard the plastic wrap. Brush the enchiladas again with the sauce and replace the foil. Turn the oven to 375° and place enchiladas on the middle rack. Bake 15 to 35 minutes, 35 minutes if refrigerated prior to baking.

Heat the sauce separately. If serving buffet style, add the sauce and garnish to the baking dish or lift out individual servings and add sauce and garnish to each serving.

ACCOMPANIMENTS

Traditional accompaniments for enchiladas are rice and beans. Bean recipes include black beans, pinto beans, or a colorful combination of beans. With red sauces, for example, colorful vegetables or a salad would be a good choice. For some of the heartier enchiladas with cheese, you might make a combination plate and serve one enchilada per person along with a chalupa or crispy taco and Tequila Orange Salad (p. 69).

Many of the salsas provide a colorful, light accompaniment. Tomato salsas go with almost anything, as do their variations with black beans, avocado, or corn. Corn or mango salsas go well with tomatillo sauces or red sauces. Tomato-based salsas offer a fresh contrast to cheese sauces.

GARNISHES

Fresh, colorful garnishes are suggested for all enchiladas. They provide contrast in texture and create visual appeal. Many traditional Southwest dishes, particularly those with red chile sauces, pinto beans, and Spanish rice, create a colorless or monochromatic plate. A small lettuce and tomato salad topped with crisp tortilla strips or a simple combination of corn, jicama, and lime do wonders for enchiladas. A single enchilada can also accompany a meat or chicken entrée. For more ideas and information about garnishes, see pages 4–6.

Several fillings and sauces follow. Mix and match them according to personal taste, but do not be limited by these sauces. The Ranchero Sauce (p. 159) goes well with chicken or beef fillings. Tomatillo Sauce (p. 158) is equally good on Shellfish Enchiladas (p. 161), and the Sour Cream Sauce (p. 157) goes well with chicken, seafood, or wild mushroom fillings. The Cornmeal Crepes (p. 15) are also good with a variety of fillings and sauces. I particularly like these for stacked enchiladas, where fillings are layered between the crepes and served stacked instead of rolled.

MILD TOMATO ENCHILADA SAUCE

MAKES 2½ CUPS

Use 1½ to 2 cups for 10 enchiladas (5 servings).

Making a homemade enchilada sauce is easier than you might think, and the results are far superior to the canned varieties. You can omit the small amount of low-fat sausage, but it gives significant flavor for less than 25 calories and a gram of fat. Either the Smoked Turkey Stock (p. 14) or Fat-Free Stock (p. 13) is excellent for making enchilada sauces, and you will need nothing else to achieve full flavor.

Advance Preparation: The sauce may be made 1 to 2 days in advance.

Coat a saucepan with a vegetable-oil cooking spray and place over medium heat. Add sausage, garlic, onion, and carrot, and cook a few minutes. Add chili powder and about ½ cup beef or chicken broth and simmer, stirring constantly about a minute. Transfer the sauce to a blender. Add the tomatoes or tomato sauce and blend until smooth. Pour the blended sauce and remaining beef or chicken broth back in the same saucepan.

Dissolve the cornstarch in the water and vinegar, and stir into the sauce. Cook 2 to 3 minutes or until thickened. Cool and season to taste with salt. Thin sauce if necessary with chicken broth or, if you desire a thicker sauce, increase cornstarch to 1½ tablespoons.

Use in any recipe that calls for Tomato Enchilada Sauce.

½ ounce low-fat smoked sausage, cut into pieces

2 cloves garlic, minced

1 tablespoon chopped onion

1 tablespoon chopped carrot

4 tablespoons chili powder

1 14-ounce can beef or chicken broth, fat removed

1½ cups chopped canned tomatoes or tomato sauce

1 tablespoon cornstarch

2 tablespoons water

2 teaspoons vinegar

½–¾ teaspoon salt

NUTRITIONAL ANALYSIS (PER ½ CUP)

Calories 59 (23% from fat); Protein 2 grams;
Carbohydrates 9 grams; Fiber 2 grams; Fat 1.5 grams.

---

3 smooth-skinned, red chile pods or ancho chile pods, toasted, stemmed, and seeded

2 cloves garlic, minced

2 tablespoons chopped onion

1 tablespoon chopped carrot

1 tablespoon safflower oil

2 tablespoons chili powder

1 14½-ounce can Mexican-style tomatoes

1 14-ounce can chicken broth

2 tablespoons maple syrup

1½ tablespoons red wine vinegar

½–¾ teaspoon salt

2 tablespoons all-purpose flour

½ cup water

1 8-ounce can tomato sauce (optional)

Note: If using ancho chile pods, the sauce will be thicker and you will need only 1 tablespoon flour for thickening.

SPICY ENCHILADA SAUCE

MAKES 3½ CUPS

Use 1½ cups for 8 enchiladas (4 servings).

The smooth-skinned red chiles are what give this sauce its assertive flavors. (You will immediately understand how tomato sauce found its way into enchilada sauces.) If you have prepared the Fat-Free (p. 13) or Smoked Turkey Stock (p. 14), use this in place of the chicken broth. Both stocks give a very rich, meaty flavor to the sauces. The maple syrup and vinegar help balance the slight bitterness from the chile pods. This sauce will please aficionados of Southwest-style red sauces. Use it with fried eggs or Huevos Rancheros Casserole (p. 151) or with one of the fillings that follows. The sauce keeps well refrigerated for one week, or freeze for another use.

Advance Preparation: The sauce may be made 1 or 2 days in advance.

Preheat the oven to 300°.

Rinse the chile pods in warm water to clean and place them directly on the oven rack. Toast for 10 to 12 minutes, then turn the oven off and leave the chiles in the oven for 20 minutes. Cool and coarsely chop into small pieces. Discard seeds and stems.

Sauté the garlic, onion, and carrot in safflower oil in a medium saucepan over medium heat. Cook until softened, then stir in the chili powder and liquid from the canned tomatoes. Add the tomatoes and chile pieces and bring to a boil. Cover, turn the heat off, and let stand about 15 minutes. Transfer to a blender jar and blend until smooth.

Return the sauce to the same saucepan and add chicken broth, maple syrup, vinegar, and salt. Dissolve the flour in the water, stirring to remove all lumps, and add to the chile mixture. Bring to a simmer, stirring constantly until thickened, about 3 minutes. Taste and adjust salt. If you prefer more tomato taste and less heat, stir in tomato sauce.

NUTRITIONAL ANALYSIS (PER ½ CUP)

Calories 92 (35% from fat); Protein 2 grams;
Carbohydrates 13 grams; Fiber 2 grams; Fat 3.5 grams.

SOUR CREAM SAUCE

MAKES 1½ CUPS

There is no sour cream in this sauce, but it has a "sour cream" flavor. Traditional sour cream enchiladas are loaded with both sour cream and melted cheese, adding up to major fat grams and calories. If you use the processed American cheese, the result is more like a cheese sauce.

Heat the butter and shallots in a small saucepan over medium heat and cook until shallots are softened. Add flour and 3 to 4 tablespoons chicken broth. Stir until the flour mixture is smooth. Add the remaining chicken broth and buttermilk. Stir constantly over medium heat until thickened, about 2 or 3 minutes. Cool a few minutes, then pour into a blender and blend until smooth.

Return to the same saucepan and stir in the cream cheese, and jack or American cheese.

Season to taste with salt and pepper.

1 tablespoon light butter

2 shallots, minced

2 tablespoons all-purpose flour

⅔ cup chicken broth

1 cup low-fat buttermilk

1 ounce light or low-fat cream cheese

1½ ounces low-fat Monterey jack cheese or 1½ ounces processed American cheese

salt and pepper

NUTRITIONAL ANALYSIS (PER ⅓ CUP)

Calories 115 (51% from fat); Protein 6 grams;
Carbohydrates 7 grams; Fiber less than 1 gram; Fat 6.5 grams.

Tomatillo Sauce

2 cloves garlic, minced

1 cup onion, diced

1 tablespoon safflower oil

10–12 tomatillos, husked, rinsed, and quartered

½ cup cilantro sprigs, stems removed

5 parsley sprigs

3 serrano chiles, stemmed, seeded

½–1 cup chicken broth

½–1 teaspoon salt coarse ground black pepper

pinch sugar substitute

Filling

5 chicken breast halves, on the bone

2–3 tablespoons chicken broth

1 cup diced fresh tomatoes

salt and pepper

10 corn tortillas

Garnishes

1 cup Crema (p. 21) or light sour cream

3 ounces feta cheese, crumbled

8 radishes, thinly sliced

CHICKEN ENCHILADAS WITH TOMATILLO SAUCE

SERVES 5

In San Antonio, these are called Green Chicken Enchiladas. In some areas, they are called Enchiladas Suizas. Recipes vary from cook to cook, but in all cases the sauce is practically fat free.

Advance Preparation: Both the sauce and chicken may be prepared a day ahead.

Preheat the oven to 400°.

To make the sauce, place a saucepan over medium heat and cook the garlic and onion in the safflower oil until translucent. You may need to add a little chicken broth to prevent browning:

In several batches, put the tomatillos, cilantro, parsley, and serrano chiles in a blender jar and blend smooth.

Add the blended tomatillos and remaining chicken broth to the saucepan and bring to a boil. Season to taste with salt, pepper, and a pinch of sugar substitute.

Season the chicken with salt and pepper and bake in the oven with the skin on for about 35 minutes. When cool enough to handle, remove the skin and bones. Shred or cut the chicken into small pieces. Moisten the chicken with the chicken broth, add tomatoes, and season with salt and pepper.

Soften the tortillas in a microwave oven or hot skillet (see p. 152). Fill with chicken mixture, roll, and seal.

Spoon some of the Tomatillo Sauce over the tortillas, then cover and bake at 350° for 15 to 20 minutes or until heated through. Heat the remaining sauce separately. Serve two enchiladas per person, and spoon additional sauce on top. Garnish each serving with a spoonful of the Crema or sour cream, feta cheese, and radishes.

NUTRITIONAL ANALYSIS (PER ENCHILADA GARNISHED, WITHOUT TOMATILLO SAUCE)
Calories 260 (29% from fat); Protein 31 grams;
Carbohydrates 15 grams; Fiber 2 grams; Fat 8.5 grams.

NUTRITIONAL ANALYSIS (TOMATILLO SAUCE, PER SERVING)
Calories 38 (47% from fat); Protein less than 1 gram;
Carbohydrates 4 grams; Fiber 1 gram; Fat 2 grams.

SPINACH ENCHILADAS RANCHERO

SERVES 5

The Ranchero Sauce is mild but has the distinctive, rich taste of poblano chiles. The sauce is excellent on almost any enchilada, omelet, or egg dish. Try using the Cornmeal Crepes (p. 15) in place of corn tortillas for a light luncheon entrée.

Advance Preparation: The sauce may be made a day in advance. The filling is best when made the day you plan to serve the enchiladas.

To prepare the sauce, rinse chiles and cut into 1-inch strips. Set aside.

In a saucepan, heat the garlic and onion in safflower oil over medium heat and cook until softened. Add the tomatoes, tomato sauce, vinegar, and reserved chiles. Bring to a simmer and cook, uncovered, 6 to 8 minutes. Add oregano, basil, salt, and pepper.

To make the filling, sear the onion in a saucepan coated with a vegetable-oil cooking spray. Add chicken broth, red bell pepper, and mushrooms and cook until softened. Stir in the ricotta cheese, spinach, cayenne pepper, and white pepper. Remove from heat and set aside.

Prepare the tortillas according to directions on p. 158. Fill with spinach mixture, roll, and seal. Bake according to method of choice.

Serve two enchiladas per person. Spoon Ranchero Sauce on top and garnish with crumbled feta cheese.

Ranchero Sauce
2 large poblano chiles, roasted, peeled and seeded
2 cloves garlic, minced
1 red onion, chopped
1 tablespoon safflower oil
1 14½-ounce can Mexican-style tomatoes
1 8-ounce can tomato sauce
1 teaspoon red wine vinegar
½ teaspoon oregano
1 tablespoon fresh basil
½–1 teaspoon salt
¼ teaspoon cracked black pepper

Filling
1 cup diced onion
4 tablespoons chicken broth
½ cup diced red bell pepper
½ cup finely chopped mushrooms
⅔ cup low-fat ricotta cheese
1 16-ounce package frozen spinach, thawed and drained
¼ teaspoon cayenne pepper
¼ teaspoon white pepper
10 corn tortillas

Garnish
3 ounces feta cheese, crumbled

NUTRITIONAL ANALYSIS (PER ENCHILADA GARNISHED, WITHOUT RANCHERO SAUCE)

Calories 114 (28% from fat); Protein 5 grams;
Carbohydrates 16 grams; Fiber 3 grams; Fat 3.5 grams.

NUTRITIONAL ANALYSIS (RANCHERO SAUCE, PER ½ CUP)

Calories 46 (29% from fat); Protein 1 gram;
Carbohydrates 9 grams; Fiber 2 grams; Fat 1.5 grams.

(continued)

low-carb

1 shallot minced

1½ cups chopped shrimp

salt and pepper

1 ounce dry vermouth

Sour Cream Sauce (p. 157)
   or Queso (p. 41)

Pico de Gallo (p. 28)

VARIATION: SHRIMP AND SPINACH ENCHILADAS

Fresh chopped shrimp are delicious with the spinach and vegetables. Choose from Sour Cream Sauce or Queso and serve with Pico de Gallo.

Sauté the shrimp and shallot in a medium skillet using a vegetable-oil cooking spray. Season with salt and pepper. Deglaze the pan with vermouth and set aside. Stir into the spinach filling.

Ladle the Sour Cream Sauce, Queso, or Pico de Gallo over the enchiladas, serving 2 per person.

SHELLFISH ENCHILADAS

SERVES 8

Almost any combination of shellfish may be used to make enchiladas with equally good results. Lobster and crab are particularly good and make a special dish for entertaining.

Heat the butter in a large skillet over medium heat. Add chiles, scallions, shallots, red bell pepper, and shellfish. Sauté, tossing constantly, 2 to 3 minutes. Season with salt and cayenne pepper.

Add white wine, lemon juice, and chicken broth and bring to a boil. Remove and strain the cooking juices from the shellfish.

Set shellfish aside and return juices to the skillet and place over medium heat. Add the cream cheese and American cheese and stir until cheese is melted and smooth.

Combine the cheese mixture with shellfish and spinach in a mixing bowl. Season with salt and pepper. Soften Cornmeal Crepes in a microwave oven. Fill each one with the shellfish mixture, roll up, and place seam side down in two 7 × 11 casserole dishes. Cover with foil.

Put the Grilled Tomato Salsa or Tomatillo Sauce in a saucepan and bring to a boil. Reduce the heat and simmer, stirring occasionally, for 5 minutes. Thin if necessary with a little chicken stock.

Preheat the oven to 400°. Heat the enchiladas, covered with foil, about 20 to 25 minutes. Serve two per person, topped with the Grilled Tomato Salsa or Tomatillo Sauce. Garnish the enchiladas with tortilla strips, whole shrimp, and Italian parsley.

**NUTRITIONAL ANALYSIS
(PER ENCHILADA, WITHOUT GARNISHES)**

Calories 87 (36% from fat); Protein 4 grams;
Carbohydrates 10 grams; Fiber less than 1 gram; Fat 3.5 grams.

---

1 tablespoon light butter

4 jalapeño chiles, stemmed, seeded, and diced

3 scallions, sliced (green and white parts)

2 shallots, minced

¼ cup diced red bell pepper

¾ pound shrimp, peeled, deveined

¾ pound lump crabmeat, shells removed, or substitute ¾ pound bay scallops for ¾ pound crabmeat

salt

¼ teaspoon cayenne pepper

½ cup white wine

1 tablespoon fresh lemon juice

2 tablespoons chicken broth

3 ounces light or low-fat cream cheese

1 ounce light processed American cheese

2 cups julienned spinach

salt and pepper

16 Cornmeal Crepes (p. 15)

Grilled Tomato Salsa (p. 30) or Tomatillo Sauce (p. 34)

Garnishes

toasted tortilla strips

cooked shrimp, tails on

Italian parsley

1 large onion, chopped

10 corn tortillas

6 ounces low-fat longhorn
  cheddar cheese

6 ounces low-fat Monterey
  jack cheese, grated

Chile Enchilada Sauce
  (p. 163)

Garnishes

4 ounces low-fat feta cheese,
  crumbled

2 ounces low-fat cheddar
  cheese, grated

1 bunch scallions, green and
  white parts, sliced

CHEESE ENCHILADAS WITH CHILE

MAKES 10 ENCHILADAS, SERVES 5

Low-fat cheeses help reduce the fat grams and calories in this Southwest favorite. Significant amounts of fat are also saved by omitting the traditional step of dipping the tortillas in oil prior to rolling. For the best results, use thin corn tortillas.

Advance preparation: Both sauce and filling may be prepared in advance.

Place a skillet over medium heat and coat with a vegetable-oil cooking spray. Add onion and cook 2 to 3 minutes until softened and lightly browned. Set aside.

Soften and seal the tortillas as described on page 158. Fill each one with a spoonful of onion and both cheeses. Roll up and place seam side down in a baking dish. Repeat, filling all the tortillas.

Heat or bake the enchiladas according to one of the methods on page 158. Serve two enchiladas per person. Spoon the Chile Enchilada Sauce on top and garnish with cheese and scallions.

**NUTRITIONAL ANALYSIS
(PER ENCHILADA, WITHOUT SAUCE)**

Calories 175 (36% from fat); Protein 13 grams;
Carbohydrates 15 grams; Fiber 2 grams; Fat 7 grams.

CHILE ENCHILADA SAUCE

MAKES 2½ CUPS SAUCE

Place a saucepan over medium heat. Add the beef and sear until well browned. Add the onion, garlic, and chili powder, stirring to break up clumps of meat. Add the beef broth and tomato sauce or tomatoes and simmer 4 to 5 minutes.

To thicken the sauce, stir the flour into ¼ cup water until smooth and free of lumps. Add a little of the hot sauce to the flour, then add the flour to the sauce, and cook 5 to 6 minutes, stirring constantly. Season with salt. Serve with Cheese Enchiladas (p. 162).

½ pound top round, ground

½ cup diced onion

2 cloves garlic, minced

3 tablespoons chili powder

1 14-ounce can beef broth

1 8-ounce can tomato sauce or 1½ cups diced tomatoes, puréed

1 tablespoon all-purpose flour

¼ cup water

¾–1 teaspoon salt

NUTRITIONAL ANALYSIS (PER ½ CUP)
Calories 175 (41% from fat); Protein 15 grams;
Carbohydrates 10 grams; Fiber 2 grams; Fat 8 grams.

Sauce

2 shallots, minced

1 clove garlic, minced

¼ cup dry white wine or vermouth

1 tablespoon finely diced carrot

1 tablespoon finely diced celery

1 tablespoon finely diced green bell pepper

1 14-ounce can chicken broth

4 tablespoons all-purpose flour

1 cup skim milk

1 teaspoon salt

¼ teaspoon white pepper

2 jalapeño chiles, stemmed, seeded, and minced

2 ounces light processed cheese or 2 ounces light or low-fat cream cheese

Chicken

1 large onion, diced

½ cup diced red bell pepper

½ cup diced green bell pepper

1 4½-ounce can diced green chiles

salt and pepper

1 10-ounce package corn tortillas, quartered and toasted

8 cooked skinless boneless chicken breast halves, diced

1 teaspoon chili powder

6 ounces low-fat Monterey jack cheese, grated

1 10-ounce can diced tomatoes and green chiles

KING RANCH CHICKEN
SERVES 8–10

Every Texan has some variation of this popular casserole dish—a sort of Enchilada Casserole. It is usually made with a canned soup and enormous amounts of cheese. This version has been lightened by making a lighter sauce and using a low-fat cheese.

Preheat the oven to 350°.

To make the sauce, put the shallots, garlic, white wine or vermouth, carrot, celery, bell peppers, and chicken broth in a saucepan over high heat and bring to a boil. Boil a few minutes, then strain, discarding vegetables and reserving the liquid. Return the liquid to the same saucepan.

Dissolve the flour in skim milk, then pour milk slowly into the hot chicken broth, stirring constantly. Reduce the heat to medium-low and cook, stirring, until thickened. Add salt, pepper, minced jalapeño chiles, and processed cheese or cream cheese. Stir sauce until the cheese is melted. Set aside.

Coat a medium saucepan with a vegetable-oil cooking spray. Over medium heat, sauté the onion, bell peppers, and chiles until softened. Season with salt and pepper and set aside.

Coat the tortilla quarters with a butter-flavored cooking spray on both sides and place on cookie sheets. Toast in a preheated 350° oven 8 minutes. Tortillas will not be crisp. Put half the tortillas in a 9 × 13 casserole.

Put half the chicken on top of the tortillas and season with salt, pepper, and chili powder. Top with half the onion, bell peppers, and chiles. Repeat the layers and pour the reserved sauce over all. Top with grated cheese and undrained diced tomatoes and green chiles.

Bake at 350° for 40 to 45 minutes or until hot.

NUTRITIONAL ANALYSIS
(PER SERVING, BASED ON TEN SERVINGS)

Calories 390 (23% from fat); Protein 53 grams;
Carbohydrates 22 grams; Fiber 2 grams; Fat 10 grams.

NANCY'S ENCHILADA CASSEROLE

SERVES 6

My friend and food aficionado Nancy Dedman designed a women's club luncheon with this as an entrée. It was served with a light green salad and miniature corn muffins. This version had one-third fewer calories and fat grams than the original and tested equally well with ground turkey or beef.

Cut five tortillas in thirds, then in thin strips, and spray with a butter-flavored spray. Toast in a 350° oven for about 8 to 10 minutes or until crisp. Set aside for garnish.

Place a medium skillet, preferably nonstick, over medium heat. One at a time, spray 7 corn tortillas with a butter-flavored spray. Using tongs, heat them on both sides in the skillet, turning often until softened. Place into 10-inch pie pan overlapping tortillas.

To make the sauce, generously coat a saucepan with a vegetable-oil cooking spray and cook the onion and mushrooms over medium heat, stirring constantly. Add the cayenne pepper, stir briefly, then add the chicken broth and bring to a boil. Dissolve the flour in skim milk and stir to remove all lumps. Add a little of the hot broth to the flour and stir in, then add the flour mixture to the broth and cook, stirring constantly, about 3 to 4 minutes. Add cream cheese, garlic salt, green chiles, and salt to taste. Stir to combine and set aside.

To cook the meat, heat the skillet again over medium heat. Add the beef and break up with a fork but allow it to sear until browned. Add garlic and onion and mix in well. Stir in the chili powder, spinach, and tomatoes. Season to taste with salt and pepper. Remove from the heat and stir in the egg substitute and 2 ounces of the cheese. Put the beef on top of the prepared tortillas. Sprinkle with half the toasted tortillas, then the reserved sauce. Top with remaining cheese. Bake in a 325° oven for 30 minutes. Garnish with remaining crisp tortillas on top.

Garnish

12 corn tortillas, divided use

Sauce

3 tablespoons chopped onion

¼ cup chopped mushrooms

⅛ teaspoon cayenne pepper

1½ cups chicken broth

4 tablespoons all purpose flour

½ cup skim milk

3 ounces light or low-fat cream cheese

¼ teaspoon garlic salt

1 4½-ounce can diced green chiles

salt

Meat

1 pound lean ground beef

2 cloves garlic, minced

1½ cups chopped onion

1 tablespoon chili powder

½ 10-ounce package frozen spinach, thawed

⅔ cup Mexican-style diced tomatoes, without juice, chopped

salt and pepper

egg substitute equivalent to 1 egg

5 ounces low-fat cheddar cheese, grated

NUTRITIONAL ANALYSIS
(PER SERVING, WITHOUT GARNISH)
Calories 359 (41% from fat); Protein 35 grams;
Carbohydrates 17 grams; Fiber 3 grams; Fat 16.5 grams.

3 corn tortillas, cut into thin
  strips

1 tablespoon light butter

1 cup diced onion

1 4½-ounce can diced green
  chiles or 1 poblano chile,
  roasted, peeled, and diced

¼ cup diced green bell
  pepper

½ cup diced tomatoes

egg substitute equivalent to
  10 eggs

½ teaspoon salt

¼ teaspoon white pepper

Garnishes

4 corn tortillas, steamed

Pico de Gallo (p. 28) or
  Quick Winter Salsa
  (p. 32)

Mashed Beans (p. 18) or
  Jalepeño Cheese Grits
  (p. 179)

MIGAS

SERVES 4

This South Texas dish probably evolved from a thrifty cook's use of leftover tortillas. I've omitted the traditional cheese and sausage and used an egg substitute to lower fat and calories. This is a fun breakfast to serve to out-of-town guests or for a brunch with friends.

Preheat the oven to 350°.

Place the tortilla strips on a cookie sheet and coat with a butter-flavored cooking spray. Toast for 8 minutes or until crisp.

In a large skillet, heat the butter over medium heat. Add the onion and sauté a few minutes to soften. Add chiles, bell pepper, tomatoes, eggs, salt, and pepper. Cook to "soft scramble" the eggs. Before they begin to set, add the toasted tortilla strips and mix in.

Serve the eggs with soft, warm tortillas and salsa of choice, Mashed Beans, or Jalapeño Grits.

**NUTRITIONAL ANALYSIS
(PER SERVING, WITHOUT GARNISHES)**

Calories 171 (13% from fat); Protein 20 grams;
Carbohydrates 17 grams; Fiber 2 grams; Fat 2.5 grams.

TURKEY AZTECA

SERVES 4

Here is another delicious way to enjoy turkey—especially the dark meat.

Coat a skillet with a vegetable-oil cooking spray and sauté the mushrooms, onion, bell peppers, and zucchini 2 to 3 minutes. Season with salt and a pinch of cayenne pepper.

Using 3 crepes per person, assemble as follows. Top one crepe with the cooked vegetables. Add a second crepe and top with turkey and enough Mild Tomato Enchilada Sauce to moisten thoroughly. Top with the third crepe, cover, and bake at 350° or microwave on high until warm. Serve topped with remaining sauce and garnish with grated cheese and fresh cilantro.

12 mushrooms, sliced

½ cup diced red onion

¼ cup diced red bell pepper

¼ cup diced green bell pepper

½ cup diced zucchini

salt

pinch cayenne pepper

12 Cornmeal Crepes (p. 15)

2 cups cooked diced turkey

1½ cups Mild Tomato Enchilada Sauce, heated (p. 155)

2 ounces low-fat Monterey jack cheese, grated

fresh minced cilantro

NUTRITIONAL ANALYSIS (PER SERVING)

Calories 421 (28% from fat); Protein 38 grams;
Carbohydrates 38 grams; Fiber 6 grams; Fat 13 grams.

8

Accompaniments

Vegetables are a beautiful part of a meal when they are fresh, tender, and used in exciting new ways.

—Albert Stockli

Traditional Tex-Mex plates always include refried beans and rice, both healthful foods that are just as easy (and just as delicious) when prepared with less fat and enhanced with vegetables. Southwest cuisine has moved away from a Tex-Mex "plate," moving toward grilled and smoked entrées, using vegetables and accompaniments in new, creative ways.

Vegetables take on a new personality when grilled over charcoal and are so flavorful you'll not want to use butter. Beans don't have to be limited to refried pinto beans. Black beans or a combination of beans, corn, and vegetables make a light accompaniment that tastes hearty.

You will not find any pasta, white potato, or very many starches in this section. While it is impractical to think one will never eat these high-carb foods, I do believe limiting them allows a lower-fat, lower-carb lifestyle. A colorful assortment of vegetables replaces most starches with the exception of a few rice dishes, including wild rice. Surprisingly, sweet potatoes have fewer carbs and calories than white potatoes and make a delicious accompaniment to many meat dishes.

In this section you'll find several cornbread recipes that vary from mini muffins and jalapeño cornbread to a moist, creamy spoon bread made with fresh corn and green chiles. These dishes will enhance both the taste and presentation of all your Southwest favorites, and your friends will be delighted to find some light alternatives.

GRILLED VEGETABLES

SERVES 4

Grilling vegetables is probably the easiest thing you'll ever do. The secret is to keep it simple. Select the freshest vegetables possible, season them well with salt and pepper, and grill over a hot fire.

Advance Preparation: Vegetables may be grilled in advance. In this case, grill them until just barely tender. Reheat the vegetables under the broiling element of your oven, 8 inches from the element, for 1 to 2 minutes. For best results, place the vegetables in a preheated pan.

Blanch carrot slices in boiling, salted water for 2 to 3 minutes or until tender but still crisp. Blanch asparagus the same way, but for just 1 minute. Blanch corn for 5 minutes.

Preheat an outdoor grill to make a hot fire.

Brush all of the vegetables generously with olive oil on both sides and season with salt and pepper. Grill on one side until marked. (You may need to drizzle a little oil on the fire to create a flame.) Turn the vegetables, brush again with olive oil, and grill on the opposite side. Vegetables should have good markings and be tender when pierced with a fork.

Place grilled vegetables on a baking sheet and keep warm in a 300° oven until ready to serve. Check seasoning and add more salt and pepper if necessary.

2 large carrots, sliced
  diagonally

1 bunch thick, fresh
  asparagus

1 large fresh corn on the
  cob, halved

light olive oil

salt and pepper

2 medium zucchini, sliced
  diagonally

3 yellow squash, sliced
  diagonally

1 red bell pepper, cut into
  strips 1-inch wide

1 yellow bell pepper, cut
  into strips 1-inch wide

NUTRITIONAL ANALYSIS (PER SERVING)
Calories 119 (23% from fat); Protein 5 grams;
Carbohydrates 18 grams; Fiber 4 grams; Fat 3 grams.

4 bunches large scallions
coarse salt
juice from 1 lime

Garnishes
diced tomatoes
lime wedges

GRILLED SCALLIONS
SERVES 6

This is probably the easiest recipe in the entire book and one sure to please onion aficionados. If you are able to buy the giant scallions (often available in South Texas), they are the best. We eat these with our fingers, but some people may prefer a knife and fork. Grilled scallions are a good garnish for almost any grilled entrée such as fajitas, chicken, or shrimp.

Preheat an outdoor grill to the highest setting.

Trim the whiskers from the scallions, clean well, and cut away bruised or brown ends. Leave about 3 inches of the green portion.

Lightly coat the scallions with a vegetable-oil cooking spray and sprinkle with coarse ground salt. Grill on both sides 1 to 2 minutes or until marked by the grill. Squeeze fresh lime juice over the scallions.

Mound the scallions on the center of a plate and garnish with fresh diced tomatoes on top. Serve lime wedges with each serving.

NUTRITIONAL ANALYSIS
(PER SERVING, WITHOUT GARNISHES)
Calories 65 (5% from fat); Protein 3 grams;
Carbohydrates 15 grams; Fiber 5 grams; Fat less than 1 gram.

SEARED SPINACH

SERVE 4

When limiting carbs, it is always a challenge to replace starches, especially when entertaining. This stir-fry makes a good base for grilled fish or chicken.

Place a large sauté pan over medium-high heat. Coat pan with an olive-oil cooking spray. Add mushrooms and pepper. Sauté until mushrooms are lightly browned. Add corn, cook a few minutes, stirring constantly, then remove vegetables. Clean the pan, coat again with spray, and place over medium-high heat. Add the olive oil and when it is hot, add the spinach in several batches. The spinach looks as if it will never fit in the pan, but don't worry, it will wilt quickly. Stir-fry briefly until wilted. This takes less than a minute. Add the mushroom mixture and toss to combine.

This needs to be prepared just prior to serving, but if your ingredients are ready, it is a very quick process.

8 mushrooms, cleaned and thinly sliced

½ red bell pepper, cut into short strips

½ cup fresh corn kernels

1 tablespoon olive oil

1 16-ounce bag fresh baby spinach

salt and pepper

NUTRITIONAL ANALYSIS (PER SERVING)
Calories 92 (39% from fat); Protein 4 grams;
Carbohydrates 10 grams; Fiber 4 grams; Fat 4 grams.

OVEN-ROASTED ASPARAGUS

SERVES 4

1½ bunches thick asparagus, about 1½ pounds

2 tablespoons olive oil

freshly ground sea salt

freshly ground pepper

Most of the oil in this recipe is not absorbed by the asparagus. You can always use an olive-oil cooking spray to reduce the amount used.

Preheat the oven to 350°.

Clean asparagus and trim woody ends.

Using a pastry brush, lightly brush asparagus with olive oil. Place in a single layer on a cookie sheet with sides and sprinkle with salt and pepper.

Bake 12 to 15 minutes or until tender when pierced with a fork. Serve immediately.

**NUTRITIONAL ANALYSIS
(PER SERVING, BASED ON
1½ POUNDS ASPARAGUS PER RECIPE)**

Calories 100 (67% from fat); Protein 3 grams;
Carbohydrates 6 grams; Fiber 2 grams; Fat 7.5 grams.

OVEN-ROASTED ONIONS

SERVES 5–6

low-fat, low-carb

I prepare this easy recipe with almost any steak, pork, or beef dish. You can use any size small onion; however, once you peel them, you will try to find onions that are the size of golf balls.

Preheat the oven to 350°.

To make the onions, use a sharp knife to remove the peel, leaving most of the core intact. Place onions in a bowl and toss with olive oil, salt, pepper, and rosemary if using.

Coat a small roasting pan with an olive-oil cooking spray. Place onions in a single layer and bake for 30 to 35 minutes, or until browned, caramelized, and tender when pierced with a fork.

Combine chicken bouillon seasoning with ¼ cup water. Heat in a microwave oven for a few seconds to dissolve. Add to the roasting pan and roast a few more minutes. This creates a little onion "jus" that you can add to whatever sauce you have made.

20 boiling onions
  (golf ball–sized)
1 tablespoon olive oil
coarse salt
coarse pepper
minced fresh rosemary
  (optional)
1 teaspoon chicken bouillon
  seasoning
¼ cup water

NUTRITIONAL ANALYSIS (PER SERVING, BASED ON 6 SERVINGS PER RECIPE)

Calories 63 (36% from fat); Protein 2 gram;
Carbohydrates 8 grams; Fiber 1 gram; Fat 2.5 grams.

¾ cup roasted and peeled
  red bell peppers (about
  1½ peppers)

⅓ cup picante sauce

¼ cup chicken broth

1 large head cauliflower,
  separated into medium-
  sized florets

½ teaspoon salt

coarse salt and pepper

additional chicken broth
  as needed

OVEN-ROASTED CAULIFLOWER

SERVES 4–6

Oven-roasted vegetables have more flavor and substance than boiled vegetables. You can use a purchased picante sauce to make this preparation easier.

Preheat oven to 375°.

Using a food processor fitted with the metal blade, or a blender, process red bell peppers with picante sauce and chicken broth to make a chunky texture. Set aside.

Fill a large saucepan with water, place over high heat, and bring to a boil. Add cauliflower and salt, cover, and boil about one minute to blanch. Remove and drain completely.

Coat a roasting pan with an olive-oil cooking spray. Add cauliflower and coat with the spray. Roast the cauliflower, covered, about 12 minutes. Uncover, top with the red pepper mixture, and roast another 5 to 10 minutes, uncovered, or until tender. Season to taste with salt and pepper. If cauliflower appears dry, add about ¼ cup chicken broth to the roasting pan.

NUTRITIONAL ANALYSIS (PER SERVING, BASED ON 4 SERVINGS PER RECIPE)
Calories 44 (5% from fat); Protein 2 grams;
Carbohydrates 4 grams; Fiber 4 grams; Fat less than 1 gram.

CONFETTI BEANS

SERVES 6–8

This combination of beans is not only good for you, but it makes a satisfying accompaniment to a simple grilled fish such as salmon, swordfish, snapper, or tuna. Use any combination of beans or peas.

Heat the butter in a large saucepan over medium heat. Add the garlic, red onion, bell peppers, and chiles and sauté until softened.

Add chicken broth and the liquid drained from the peas or northern beans. Bring to a boil and reduce to thicken the liquids. Add the peas and the beans and heat through.

Add the thyme, cilantro, and tomatoes. Season with salt and pepper.

NUTRITIONAL ANALYSIS (PER SERVING, BASED ON EIGHT SERVINGS)

Calories 113 (20% from fat); Protein 5 grams; Carbohydrates 18 grams; Fiber 5 grams; Fat 2.5 grams.

---

1 tablespoon light butter

2 garlic cloves, minced

1 cup diced red onion

½ cup diced green bell pepper

½ cup diced red bell pepper

2 tablespoons diced pickled jalapeño chiles

¼–½ cup chicken broth

1 cup field or black-eyed peas, drained

1 cup northern beans, drained

1 cup black beans, drained

pinch of thyme

1 tablespoon minced fresh cilantro

1 cup peeled and diced tomatoes

salt and pepper

5 sweet potatoes, about
    3¼ pounds

½ yellow onion, cut into
    pieces

2 tablespoons light butter

1 tablespoon orange juice

1 tablespoon chipotle chile
    adobo sauce

salt

CHIPOTLE MASHED SWEET POTATOES

SERVES 6-8

A small amount of chipotle seasoning or adobo sauce goes a long way, but when used with restraint, adds a smoky flavor that is delicious with sweet potatoes. I prefer to use just the adobo sauce in this recipe. One white baked potato has about 220 calories and 51 carbs while a sweet potato has 118 calories and about 27 carbs. Both have practically no fat.

Advance Preparation: Whipped sweet potatoes can be made a day in advance and reheated in a 350° oven for 30 minutes. They tend to leak water, so you will need to stir through them to incorporate the liquid.

Preheat oven to 350°.

Peel the sweet potatoes and cut into chunks. You will have about 9 cups. Put potatoes and onion in a large saucepan, adding enough water to cover the vegetables. Bring the water to a boil, reduce the heat, and simmer for 20 to 25 minutes or until potatoes are tender. Drain in a colander.

Using a food processor fitted with the metal blade, process half the sweet potatoes and onion with butter, orange juice, and chipotle until mashed. Remove and process remaining potatoes. Combine the mixtures in a 2-quart casserole dish and season to taste with salt.

Heat the potatoes in a 350° oven for about 10 to 15 minutes.

NUTRITIONAL ANALYSIS (PER SERVING, BASED ON EIGHT SERVINGS)
Calories 118 (31% from fat); Protein 1 gram;
Carbohydrates 20 grams; Fiber 3 grams; Fat 4 grams.

ARROZ BLANCO

SERVES 6–8

This simple rice recipe goes well with enchiladas, seafood, or chicken entrées. It takes only a small amount of butter to give a buttery flavor to the rice.

Combine chicken broth, butter, water, and salt in a 2-quart saucepan and bring to a boil. Add the rice, lower the heat to medium-low and simmer, covered, for 15 minutes. Brown rice may take slightly longer.

Coat a medium skillet with a vegetable-oil cooking spray and place over medium heat. Add the onion, zucchini, and sundried tomatoes and sauté, stirring constantly, until softened. You may need to use additional spray to prevent burning. Add onion mixture and corn to the rice, replace the cover, and cook without stirring for 5 minutes.

Stir to combine rice and vegetables and adjust salt and pepper.

Garnish each serving with sliced scallions and minced parsley.

1 cup chicken broth

1 tablespoon light butter

1 cup water

1 teaspoon salt

1 cup long-grain white or brown rice

1 cup chopped onion

1 cup diced zucchini

½ cup diced sun-dried tomatoes

1 cup fresh or frozen (thawed) corn kernels

salt and pepper

Garnishes

2 tablespoons sliced scallions (green part)

1 tablespoon minced parsley

NUTRITIONAL ANALYSIS (PER SERVING, BASED ON EIGHT SERVINGS)

Calories 122 (7% from fat); Protein 3 grams; Carbohydrates 25 grams; Fiber 1 gram; Fat 1 gram.

1 tablespoon light butter

1 small onion, diced

1½ cups chicken broth

1¾ cups water

½ teaspoon salt

¼ teaspoon pepper

1 cup wild rice

2 tablespoons chopped
  pecans

2 tablespoons minced
  parsley or snipped chives

WILD PECAN RICE

MAKES 6 SERVINGS

Wild rice is low in both carbs and fat, so this accompaniment is suitable for almost any seafood, shellfish, chicken, or meat. Additionally, you can prepare the rice in advance and freeze it to use at a later time.

Advance Preparation: Prepare the rice as directed, but stir in pecans and parsley when ready to reheat and serve. Reheat, covered, in a 350° oven for about 30 minutes.

Preheat oven to 275°.

Melt the butter in a medium saucepan over medium-high heat. Add onion and sauté until softened. Add chicken broth, water, salt, pepper, and wild rice. Increase the heat to high and bring to a boil. Reduce heat to a simmer and cook, covered, for 40 to 45 minutes, or until rice is tender but not mushy. Stir in pecans and parsley or chives.

Transfer the rice to a casserole dish, cover, and keep warm in a 275° oven for at least 12 minutes or up to 20 minutes. Check a couple times, and if the rice is dry, add enough chicken broth to moisten.

NUTRITIONAL ANALYSIS (PER SERVING)

Calories 138 (13% from fat); Protein 6 grams;
Carbohydrates 24 grams; Fiber 2 grams; Fat 2 grams.

JALAPEÑO CHEESE GRITS

MAKES 7–8 SERVINGS

While traditionally a breakfast dish, grits are served at almost any meal in the Southwest. Serve them with pork, ham, veal cutlets, or the Tequila Shrimp (p. 123). When prepared in this manner, the grits are very light, soft and fluffy.

Advance preparation: Jalepeño Cheese Grits can be prepared in advance, held at room temperature, and then baked. Stir through briefly before baking.

Preheat oven to 350°.

Put the water, grits, salt, and sugar substitute in a medium saucepan. Place over medium-high heat, stirring occasionally. Once the water reaches a simmer, stir constantly. Reduce the heat to low and maintaining a simmer, cook until thick, stirring constantly, about 6 to 8 minutes.

Stir in the cheeses, butter, eggs, and jalapeño chiles and cook over low heat until cheese is just melted.

Transfer the grits to a 1½ quart casserole that has been lightly buttered.

Bake the casserole covered 20 to 25 minutes, or until the mixture is just set but still soft. Grits may be baked in individual custard cups. In this case, top with a small amount of shredded cheddar or parmesan cheese and bake uncovered for 10 minutes.

5 cups water

1¼ cups white grits (not instant)

salt

½ package sugar substitute

3 ounces Manchego or Monterey jack cheese, grated (about ¾ cups)

2 ounces light American processed cheese

1 tablespoon light butter

3 large eggs, beaten

2 tablespoons diced and seeded jalapeño chiles or ½ teaspoon cayenne pepper

---

NUTRITIONAL ANALYSIS
(PER SERVING, BASED ON 8 SERVINGS)

Calories 212 (36% from fat); Protein 9 grams; Carbohydrates 24 grams; Fiber less than 1 gram; Fat 8.5 grams.

3 cups water

1 cup chicken broth

½ cup grits (not instant)

½ cup yellow cornmeal

1 teaspoon salt

2 ounces Havarti cheese, grated

2 ounces Manchego cheese, grated

½ package sugar substitute

3 tablespoons grated parmesan cheese

CORNMEAL PUDDING
SERVES 6-8

Like a soft polenta, with the consistency of mashed potatoes, Corn-meal Pudding is another true comfort food. It pairs well with shell-fish, pork tenderloin, veal chops, or grilled salmon. I like it for enter-taining as you can make it ahead and hold it in the oven for up to 45 minutes.

Preheat oven to 200°.

Using a medium saucepan, bring water, chicken broth, grits, cornmeal, and salt to a boil over medium-high heat. Stir-ring occasionally, bring the mixture to a simmer. Reduce the heat to maintain a simmer, and stirring constantly, continue to cook until very thick, about 8 minutes.

Gradually add grated cheeses and sugar substitute, and stir until melted. The mixture will be somewhat thin.

Transfer the pudding to a 1½-quart casserole or square glass baking dish that has been coated with a butter-flavored cooking spray. Sprinkle evenly with cheese. Finish cooking and keep warm in a 200° oven, uncovered, until ready to serve, for at least 35 minutes and up to 50 minutes.

NUTRITIONAL ANALYSIS (PER SERVING, BASED ON EIGHT SERVINGS)

Calories 121 (30% from fat); Protein 6 grams;
Carbohydrates 15 grams; Fiber less than 1 gram; Fat 4 grams.

CORN AND GREEN CHILE SPOON BREAD

SERVES 8

This is one of my favorite recipes for entertaining. It holds well in a warm oven up to 30 minutes and is a wonderful accompaniment to grilled fish or poultry or to serve on a buffet table with beans. Individual servings spooned into a fringed tamale husk make an attractive presentation.

Preheat the oven to 350°.

If using fresh corn, cut the corn kernels from the cobs and set aside. If using frozen, thaw before using.

Bring the chicken broth and milk to a boil in a saucepan. Reduce the heat to low. Slowly add the cornmeal, stirring constantly, and cook until thickened, about 2 minutes. Add the corn and set aside.

Coat a medium skillet with a vegetable-oil cooking spray and place over medium heat. Add onion, bell pepper, and both chiles, and cook until softened, about 2 to 3 minutes. Add onion mixture and egg substitute to the cornmeal mixture. Season with salt and pepper to taste.

In a separate bowl, beat the egg whites with sugar until stiff. Fold some of the whites into the cornmeal to lighten the mixture. Fold lightened cornmeal mixture into the whites.

Coat a 2-quart oblong pan with a vegetable-oil cooking spray and pour the batter into the pan. Sprinkle cheese on top. Place the pan in a larger pan that has been partially filled with warm water. Bake for 45 minutes to 1 hour.

You may hold the spoon bread up to 30 minutes by turning the oven down to the lowest setting, leaving the door wide open for 5 minutes to cool down. Close the door to "hold" the pudding until ready to serve.

1½ cups fresh or frozen corn kernels

1 cup chicken broth

1 cup skim milk

½ cup yellow cornmeal

½ cup diced onion

½ cup diced red bell pepper

½ cup diced green chiles

1–2 jalapeño chiles, stemmed, seeded, and diced

egg substitute equivalent to 2 eggs

¼ teaspoon salt, to taste

⅛ teaspoon white pepper

2 egg whites

1 teaspoon sugar

1–2 tablespoons grated Romano cheese

NUTRITIONAL ANALYSIS (PER SERVING)

Calories 96 (9% from fat); Protein 6 grams;
Carbohydrates 16 grams; Fiber 1 gram; Fat 1 gram.

½ cup diced onion

1–2 jalapeño chiles, stemmed, seeded, and diced

⅔ cup all-purpose flour

1 cup yellow cornmeal

1½ tablespoons sugar

1½ teaspoon salt

4 teaspoons baking powder

2 egg whites

egg substitute equivalent to 2 eggs

1 cup skim milk

4 tablespoons light mayonnaise

JALAPEÑO CORNBREAD

MAKES 12 WEDGES

Cornbread is always best when served right after baking because it tends to dry out.

Preheat the oven to 400°.

Coat a small skillet with a vegetable-oil cooking spray and sauté the onion over medium heat until softened, about 3 to 4 minutes. Add jalapeño chile and set aside.

Combine the flour, cornmeal, sugar, salt, and baking powder in a mixing bowl.

Whip together the egg whites, egg substitute, skim milk, and mayonnaise. Add to the dry ingredients and mix well.

Coat a 9-inch round pan with a butter-flavored cooking spray. Pour the batter into the pan and spray the top lightly. Bake for 30 minutes or until puffed and cornbread pulls away from the edges of the pan. Reduce the heat to 350° and bake another 10 minutes. Serve immediately.

NUTRITIONAL ANALYSIS (PER WEDGE)
Calories 95 (14% from fat); Protein 4 grams;
Carbohydrates 17 grams; Fiber 1 gram; Fat 1.5 grams.

CORNMEAL MUFFINS

MAKES 32 MINIATURE MUFFINS
OR 12 LARGE MUFFINS

These moist muffins are delicious with salads, soups, or entrées. They reheat quite well but are best when served the same day you prepare them.

Preheat oven to 375°.

Combine the cornmeal, flour, baking powder, salt, and sugar in a bowl and stir to distribute the baking powder.

Stir the mayonnaise, egg substitute, skim milk, and corn into the dry ingredients and mix well. Coat muffin cups generously with a butter-flavored cooking spray. Fill cups ⅞ full and bake 12 to 14 minutes for miniature muffins, about 18 minutes for large muffins.

Cool in the pan 5 minutes, then remove using a sharp knife. When cool, store the muffins in sealed bags. Reheat in a 400° oven or microwave when ready to serve.

⅔ cup cornmeal

½ cup all-purpose flour

2 teaspoons baking powder

1 teaspoon salt

1 tablespoon sugar

3 tablespoons light
  mayonnaise

egg substitute equivalent to
  2 eggs

½ cup skim milk

½ cup cream-style corn

NUTRITIONAL ANALYSIS
(PER MINIATURE MUFFIN)

Calories 29 (8% from fat); Protein 1 gram; Carbohydrates 5 grams; Fiber less than 1 gram; Fat less than 1 gram.

NUTRITIONAL ANALYSIS
(PER LARGE MUFFIN)

Calories 76 (8% from fat); Protein 3 grams; Carbohydrates 14 grams; Fiber less than 1 gram; Fat less than 1 gram.

9
Desserts

All's well that ends well.
—William Shakespeare

Americans have quite a sweet tooth, despite a yearning to be thin. Even the most disciplined can fall prey to chocolate or a warm berry cobbler. Something sweet is particularly satisfying after a spicy meal. Unfortunately, most low-carb desserts are high in fat and low-fat desserts are high in sugar.

While desserts are almost impossible to make low in both fats and carbs, all of the desserts in this chapter are light, and many are significantly lower in fats, carbs, and calories than most cakes, pies, ice creams, and cobblers. I have used a sugar substitute as much as possible without sacrificing taste or texture. The Decadent Chocolate Cake (p. 197) is one of my favorites and is surprisingly low in fats and carbs. When I entertain, I want a great dessert with a pretty presentation but one that won't send me to the gym for three hours.

CARAMEL FLAN

SERVES 4

This flan is much lighter than those made with condensed milk, in taste as well as calories. The cornstarch creates a slightly dense texture and is necessary when using skim milk.

Put 4 12-ounce custard cups in a 9 × 13 baking dish and fill it one-third full of water.

Heat a medium skillet over medium heat. Add water and ½ cup sugar and keep on the heat until the sugar turns amber and begins to caramelize. Shake the pan to distribute the sugar. It should melt and be amber in color but not burned. Immediately pour melted sugar in the custard cups, tilting them to coat the bottom.

Dissolve the cornstarch in ½ cup of the milk in a small saucepan, then add the remaining milk and orange peel, and bring to a simmer over medium-high heat. Stir constantly once the milk is warm.

In a separate bowl, whisk together the egg substitute, remaining sugar, and vanilla. Slowly add the milk and mix well. Divide between the custard cups.

Bake for 40 to 45 minutes or until a knife inserted in the custard confirms it is set. Remove the cups from the water bath and cool 15 minutes. Refrigerate 3 hours. Run a knife around the edge to unmold the flans.

Serve garnished with orange sections and sliced strawberries.

1 tablespoon water

¾ cup granulated sugar (divided use)

1 tablespoon cornstarch

2 cups skim milk

2 teaspoons freshly grated orange peel (no white part)

egg substitute equivalent to 4 eggs

1 teaspoon vanilla extract

Garnishes

sections from 1 orange, all membrane removed

8 strawberries, hulled and sliced

NUTRITIONAL ANALYSIS
(PER SERVING GARNISHED)

Calories 250 (2% from fat); Protein 11 grams;
Carbohydrates 51 grams; Fiber 1 gram; Fat less than 1 gram.

Custard

2 cups skim milk

1 envelope custard powder or 2½ tablespoons arrowroot

egg substitute equivalent to 4 eggs

¼ cup sugar substitute

1 tablespoon amaretto liqueur

2 teaspoons vanilla extract

Meringue

5 large egg whites, at room temperature

¼ teaspoon cream of tartar

½ cup granulated sugar

1 teaspoon vanilla extract

Caramel

2 tablespoons water

1 cup granulated sugar

Garnish

fresh seasonal berries

CARAMEL MERINGUE ALMENDRADO

SERVES 6

This recipe is adapted from Natillas, the New Mexican dessert made with egg whites and gelatin served on soft custard. The caramelized sugar is easy to do (no fat!) and makes a dramatic dessert.

To make the custard, heat 1½ cups milk in a 1-quart saucepan over medium heat. In a bowl, whisk together the custard powder or arrowroot, egg substitute, sugar, and remaining milk until smooth. Slowly add the mixture to the milk, stirring constantly. Reduce the heat to medium-low. Cook 3 to 5 minutes, lifting the pan from the heat if the mixture threatens to curdle. Stir until the custard is thickened and smooth. Add amaretto and vanilla. Strain, cool, and refrigerate.

To make the meringue, preheat the oven to 325°. In a clean bowl, beat the egg whites with cream of tartar until they hold soft peaks. Gradually add the sugar, continuing to beat. Beat until the egg whites hold stiff, glossy peaks, then fold in vanilla.

Lightly coat 6 10-ounce custard cups or soufflé dishes with a vegetable-oil cooking spray. Sprinkle lightly with sugar. Place the cups in a large pan partially filled with warm water. Spoon meringue into prepared dishes and bake for about 10 minutes. (Meringues will fall as they cool.) Run a knife around the edges of the cups and invert meringues on serving plates. Pour the chilled custard around each meringue. Refrigerate. (This should be done no more than 2 hours before serving time.)

To finish the dessert, make the caramel. Put the water and sugar for the caramel in a medium skillet over medium-high heat. Heat until the sugar melts and begins to turn amber. Once all the sugar is melted and light brown, stir briefly and remove from heat. Let the sugar cool slightly but not long enough to harden (this takes seconds). Pour the caramelized sugar in a thin stream, back and forth in both directions, to drizzle caramel over the meringues. The sugar will harden almost immediately.

Garnish with fresh berries.

**NUTRITIONAL ANALYSIS
(PER SERVING, WITHOUT GARNISH)**

Calories 274 (3% from fat); Protein 11 grams; Carbohydrates 56 grams; Fiber less than 1 gram; Fat less than 1 gram.

Shells

½ cup slivered almonds
   (1 ounce)

½ cup sugar

2–3 tablespoons water
   (more or less)

1 tablespoon corn syrup

½ cup mixed fresh
   blueberries and
   raspberries or
   strawberries (per shell)

4 tablespoons low-fat
   nondairy topping
   (per shell)

Garnishes

2 tablespoons Caramel
   Sauce (p. 199)

fresh mint sprig

2–4 fresh berries

COOKIE TACOS

MAKES 12

These crisp little shells may be made into sweet tacos or chalupas, the latter being a little easier to make. Fill them with non-fat ice cream and fresh berries and caramel or chocolate sauce, or try the following combination.

Preheat the oven to 375°.

To make the shells, put the almonds and sugar in a food processor fitted with the metal blade and process until finely chopped. Add water and corn syrup and process again. The batter should be moistened but not "soupy." Let it rest for 15 minutes.

Line cookie sheets with parchment paper. Drop round spoonfuls of batter on parchment sheets. (A miniature ice cream scoop makes uniform balls that spread evenly.) Bake 10 to 12 minutes or until balls spread and are lightly browned.

To make sweet taco shells, quickly cut around each cookie and drape over a broomstick handle to make a shell. Hold the cookie in place a few seconds until it begins to harden. If making flat chalupa shells, simply cool the rounds on parchment. Store tacos in airtight containers. Remove parchment when ready to use.

To assemble the dessert, place shells on a serving plate. If taco shells will not stand up, place a few berries on either side to hold in place. Carefully fill each shell with assorted berries and a dollop of topping. Spoon Raspberry Sauce (p. 189) on the plate and drizzle caramel over the taco.

Garnish with a mint sprig.

NUTRITIONAL ANALYSIS (PER TACO)
Calories 149 (36% from fat); Protein 1 gram;
Carbohydrates 23 grams; Fiber 5 grams; Fat 6 grams.

RASPBERRY SAUCE

Bring frozen raspberries to a boil. Add sugar substitute and boil about 2 minutes. Blend in a blender or a food processor fitted with the metal blade. Strain to remove seeds.

1 16-ounce package frozen raspberries

1–2 tablespoons sugar substitute

NUTRITIONAL ANALYSIS (PER RECIPE)

Calories 229 (8% from fat); Protein 2 grams;

Carbohydrates 53 grams; Fiber 31 grams; Fat 1 gram.

Taco Shells (p. 188)

6 scoops light vanilla ice cream or low-fat frozen yogurt

Chocolate Sauce (p. 200)

6 strawberries

CRISP ICE CREAM SANDWICH

SERVES 6

These flat, round "cookies" are easier to make than the taco "shells" and make an attractive, light dessert. Be sure to let the batter rest 5 to 10 minutes before baking. These look like an ice cream sandwich.

Prepare the shells as directed. Do not shape, but allow to cool, then peel away parchment paper.

Using a round ice cream scoop, place rounds of ice cream or frozen yogurt on parchment paper or foil. Press down in the center of each scoop to make a flat disk about the size of the shells. Freeze until ready to assemble the dessert.

To assemble, place a shell on each 9- to 10-inch plate. Place an ice cream disc on top, then top with another shell.

Drizzle warm Chocolate Sauce over the "sandwich" and garnish on top with a fresh strawberry.

NUTRITIONAL ANALYSIS (PER SANDWICH WITHOUT CHOCOLATE SAUCE)

Calories 201 (18% from fat); Protein 4 grams;
Carbohydrates 37 grams; Fiber 2 grams; Fat 4 grams.

APPLE BREAD PUDDING

SERVES 8

Mexican bread pudding was traditionally made with cheese and lots of sugar in place of an egg-milk mixture. New products make it possible to use a sugar substitute and reduce the fat in the egg-milk mixture. This has a soft, custard-like texture and is best served warm from the oven.

Preheat the oven to 325°.

Melt the butter in a medium-sized skillet over medium heat. Add the apples and simmer for 5 minutes, covered. Add ⅛ cup sugar substitute and cinnamon. Simmer another 2 minutes, uncovered.

Beat evaporated milk and egg substitute to combine. Add bread, vanilla, craisins, sugar substitute, and apples.

Lightly coat an 8 × 8 pan with butter cooking spray. Add apple bread mixture. Toss pecans in maple syrup and scatter over the top.

Bake 30 to 35 minutes or until set. Cut into squares and serve warm with a low-fat, non-dairy topping.

2 tablespoons light butter

4 granny smith apples, peeled, cored, and coarsely chopped

½ cup sugar substitute, divided use

½ teaspoon cinnamon

1⅓ cups non-fat evaporated milk

egg substitute equivalent to 2 eggs

1 cup cubed bread, about ½ inch square

½ teaspoon vanilla

⅓ cup craisins

12 pecans, toasted and chopped

1½ tablespoons sugar-free maple syrup

**NUTRITIONAL ANALYSIS
(PER SERVING, WITHOUT TOPPING)**
Calories 280 (11% from fat); Protein 5 grams;
Carbohydrates 57 grams; Fiber 3 grams; Fat 3.5 grams.

---

2 tablespoons butter

¾ cup sugar (divided use)

¼ cup sugar substitute

4 tablespoons flour

¼ teaspoon salt

5 tablespoons fresh lime
  juice

3 eggs, separated

1½ cups skim milk

Garnish

Raspberry Sauce (p. 189)
  or fresh raspberries

MEXICAN LIME SOUFFLE

MAKES 6 SERVINGS

Mexican limes make this old county fair–winner even better. The soufflé separates as it cooks, leaving a thick custard on the bottom, with a light sponge-like cake on top.

You can cook this in an 8 × 8 × 2 baking pan and then spoon it into margarita glasses with fresh raspberries, or bake it in custard cups to make individual servings.

Preheat oven to 350°.

In a large mixing bowl, cream the butter, ½ cup sugar, the sugar substitute, flour, salt, and lime juice. Add egg yolks and milk and beat until smooth. The mixture will be thin.

In a separate bowl, beat the egg whites until stiff peaks form. Gradually add the remaining ¼ cup sugar and beat to stiff peaks. Fold mixtures together.

Lightly butter 6 6-ounce custard cups. Place cups in a pan large enough to hold all six and fill with 1½ to 2 inches of warm water. Fill the cups with the lemon mixture about ⅞ full. Bake for 25 to 30 minutes. Remove and cool. Refrigerate until ready to serve.

To unmold, run a knife around the edge of the custards. Place a dessert plate on top, and turn upside down to unmold. Surround with Raspberry Sauce or fresh raspberries.

**NUTRITIONAL ANALYSIS
(PER SERVING, WITHOUT GARNISH)**

Calories 210 (28% from fat); Protein 5 grams;
Carbohydrates 33 grams; Fiber less than 1 gram; Fat 6.5 grams.

PIÑA COLADA CAKE

MAKES 10 SERVINGS

The original version of this cake was a Mexican wedding cake made with all crushed pineapple. Like many Mexican desserts it was very sweet but without butter.

Replacing most of the pineapple with apple sauce cuts back on the sugar, keeping a pineapple flavor.

Preheat oven to 350°.

In a medium-sized mixing bowl, combine the sugar, flour, and baking soda. Stir to combine.

Add coconut or rum extract, applesauce, pineapple, and pecans, and stir just enough to incorporate the flour but do not over mix.

Pour into a lightly buttered 8 × 8 × 2 baking dish. Bake for 25 to 30 minutes, or until tester confirms the cake is done. Do not overbake or cake can become dry.

Top the cooled cake with low-fat nondairy topping and chopped pecans. Refrigerate until ready to serve.

1 cup granulated sugar

1 cup flour

1 teaspoon baking soda

1 teaspoon coconut or rum extract

1 cup applesauce

⅓ cup crushed pineapple, including the juice

¼ cup chopped pecans

Topping

2 cups low-fat nondairy topping

⅓ cup chopped pecans

NUTRITIONAL ANALYSIS (PER SERVING)

Calories 200 (27% from fat); Protein 27 grams;
Carbohydrates 34 grams; Fiber 1 gram; Fat 2.5 grams.

Note: If you want to indulge, this is just as great served on a pool of caramel sauce.

Cake

2 cups sifted all-purpose
    flour

1 tablespoon baking powder

6 eggs, separated

1 cup sugar

⅓ cup 2% milk

1½ teaspoons vanilla extract

Milk

8 ounces (about ½ can) fat-
    free sweetened condensed
    milk

1½ cans (18 ounces) fat-free
    evaporated milk

1½ cup fat-free half-and-half

Meringue Topping

3 egg whites

¾ cup sugar

1 tablespoon fresh lime juice

Garnish

toasted sliced almonds

TRES LECHE CAKE
SERVES 15

This unusually moist cake has very little fat, but the original version was extremely high in sugar. I suspect butter was scarce for many Mexican cooks, so they made their cakes moist by using this method. Most bakeries use whipped cream for the icing, but you can use a low-fat nondairy topping or the meringue that follows. While Mexican in origin, this cake has become popular in mainstream American bakeries.

Advance Preparation: The cake is best when made a day in advance.

Preheat oven to 375°.

    To make the cake, coat a 9 × 11 baking pan lightly with a vegetable-oil cooking spray. Combine the flour and baking powder in a small bowl and set aside.

    Put egg whites in a large, clean bowl. Using an electric mixer beat the whites until frothy. Gradually add the sugar and continue beating until stiff peaks form, about 5 minutes. Beat in egg yolks, one at a time. Alternating, fold in flour, milk, and vanilla. Fold until all the flour is incorporated but do not over mix.

    Pour the batter into the prepared pan and bake 30 minutes, or until a toothpick test confirms cake is done. Cool ten minutes, then using a fork with sharp tines, poke holes all over the cake surface.

    To make the milk mixture, bring half the condensed milk, evaporated milk, and half-and-half to a boil in a small saucepan. Stir in the remaining milk and remove from the heat.

    Pour ¼ of the mixture slowly and evenly over the cake. When absorbed, repeat until all the liquid has been used. Chill at least 3 hours.

    Frost the cake with chilled low-fat nondairy topping, or make the following meringue.

Put the egg whites in the top of a double boiler. Fill the bottom half of the double boiler ⅓ full of water and place over medium high heat and bring the water to a simmer. Beat the egg whites over simmering water until frothy, then gradually add sugar, and continue beating until stiff, glossy peaks form. Beat in the lime juice. Spread immediately over the cooled cake and chill until ready to serve.

Garnish the cake with toasted sliced almonds.

**NUTRITIONAL ANALYSIS
(PER SERVING, WITHOUT GARNISH)**
Calories 280 (8% from fat); Protein 10 grams;
Carbohydrates 54 grams; Fiber less than 1 gram; Fat 2.5 grams.

Kahlua Sauce

¾ cup coffee

⅓ cup sugar-free maple syrup

¼ cup Kahlua

Filling

6 ounces light or low-fat cream cheese

1¼ cups canned pumpkin

¼ teaspoon cinnamon

½ cup sugar substitute

½ teaspoon vanilla extract

¾ cup non-dairy, light whipped topping

1¼ 3-oz. packages ladyfingers, without cream filling

cocoa powder

Sauce

Chocolate Sauce (p. 200)

Garnish

chocolate curls

mint sprig or fresh strawberry

KAHLUA PUMPKIN CAKE
SERVES 12

Pumpkin is a favorite ingredient for Southwest desserts. I tried many ways to "de-fat" this sweet snack, but phyllo dough became too soggy to make a satisfactory pastry, and without fat most pastry is very tough. The Italian dessert tiramisu inspired this variation that marries pumpkin, Kahlua, and chocolate in a light, low-fat dessert.

To make the sauce, combine coffee, maple syrup, and Kahlua. Set aside.

To make the filling, put the cream cheese, pumpkin, cinnamon, and sugar substitute in a a bowl and beat with a hand mixer until light and creamy. Fold in whipped topping

To assemble the dessert, split the ladyfingers and place half of them cut side up in an 8 × 11 pan. Drizzle with the Kahlua sauce to soak all the ladyfingers. Spread half the pumpkin mixture on top. Put the cocoa in a sieve and shake to lightly dust the pumpkin with cocoa. Repeat procedure, ending with cocoa powder on top. Refrigerate at least 8 hours.

To serve the dessert, pool the plate with the chocolate sauce. Cut the cake into squares and garnish the top with chocolate curls, and a mint sprig or fresh strawberry.

**NUTRITIONAL ANALYSIS
(PER SERVING, WITHOUT SAUCE)**
Calories 167 (45% from fat); Protein 3 grams;
Carbohydrates 17 grams; Fiber 1 gram; Fat 8.5 grams.

DECADENT CHOCOLATE CAKE

MAKES 10–12 WEDGES

This light, but rich chocolatey cake is made without flour or nuts and can be garnished or served in a variety of ways. Pool the plate with Raspberry Sauce (p. 189) and then drizzle the cake with a non-dairy whipped topping, or arrange fresh berries atop the cake and drizzle with chocolate sauce. It is also delicious served warm, sprinkled with powdered sugar. The illustration on page shows the cake topped with a Tequila Sabayon (p. 198). A spring form pan is essential because of the delicate, moist texture.

Preheat the oven to 350 (for this recipe it is important to set convection ovens to 325).

Bring the water and butter to a boil in a medium-sized saucepan. Add oatmeal, remove from heat and cover. Let stand 2 minutes.

Stir in 1¼ cups sugar, egg yolks, and vanilla.

In a separate, clean bowl beat the egg whites with cream of tartar until stiffened. Slowly add the remaining ¼ cup sugar and beat to stiff peaks.

Stir cocoa into the oatmeal mixture, then stir in about ⅓ of the stiff egg whites to lighten the chocolate mixture.

Combine the chocolate mixture with stiff egg whites and fold together until well mixed.

Coat a 9-inch springform pan with a vegetable coating spray. Pour the cake into the pan and bake in the middle of the oven for 45 to 50 minutes, or until cake is puffed and toothpick test confirms doneness. Cool 15 minutes before slicing.

¾ cups boiling water

1½ tablespoons light butter

6 tablespoons instant oatmeal

1½ cups sugar, divided use

4 egg yolks

1 tablespoon vanilla extract

7 egg whites

Pinch cream of tartar

¾ cups powdered, unsweetened cocoa

NUTRITIONAL ANALYSIS (PER WEDGE, BASED ON 10 WEDGES PER RECIPE)

Calories 184 (20% from fat); Protein 4 grams;
Carbohydrates 33 grams; Fiber 2 grams; Fat 4 grams.

3 whole eggs

¼ cup tequila

½ cup sugar, divided use

2 egg whites

pinch cream of tartar

Garnishes

fresh berries

1 tablespoon finely minced
 orange peel

TEQUILA SABAYON

MAKES 3½ CUPS

This classic sauce has been made with everything from Marsala to Champagne. Traditionally, the egg and sugar mixture was cooled and then finished with whipping cream. This version is finished with a meringue, making a light, foamy sauce. Unfortunately, it is difficult to make ahead, as it tends to lose volume and separate. You can always whisk the sauce to bring it back, but the texture will be denser. Only you know that . . . you don't have to announce it to your guests.

Put the eggs, tequila, and sugar in a small mixing bowl. Beat a few minutes, then place over a medium-sized saucepan of simmering (not boiling) water. Beating constantly, cook the mixture until light and frothy, about doubled in volume. This will take about 3 to 4 minutes. Turn off the heat and remove the bowl. After the water cools slightly, keep the sauce warm, over the water, covered, until you are ready to beat the egg whites and serve the sauce. If the sauce separates, just beat it again to bring it back.

In a clean mixing bowl, beat the egg whites with cream of tartar until soft peaks form. Add the sugar and beat to stiff peaks. Whip into the egg yolk mixture, still over the warm water. Serve immediately in stemmed glasses with fresh berries. Garnish with orange peel.

**NUTRITIONAL ANALYSIS
(PER ¾ CUP SERVING)**

Calories 170 (26% from fat); Protein 5 grams;
Carbohydrates 26 grams; Fiber 2 grams; Fat 5 grams.

CARAMEL SAUCE

MAKES ¾ CUP

Mexican caramel, called cajeta, is made from sugar and rich milk or cream, which is very high in fat and calories. While this version has quite a lot of sugar, the fat grams are minimal. Almost anything tastes better drizzled with a little caramel, and this goes a long way to satisfy a sweet tooth.

Heat the sugar over high heat in a small saucepan. When it begins to brown, shake the pan to distribute sugar. Do not stir until sugar becomes liquid and caramelizes.

Stir the sugar until nearly all lumps are gone and you have an amber liquid. Remove from heat and gradually add the water.

The mixture will sizzle and foam and clumps of sugar will form, but these will melt eventually. Return the saucepan to low heat and cook, stirring constantly, until nearly all lumps melt. Add condensed milk and simmer about 4 to 5 minutes.

Whisk in vanilla, then remove from the heat and cool. Stir occasionally during the cooling process.

Store at room temperature.

- ¾ cup granulated sugar
- ½–¾ cup boiling water
- 6 tablespoons non-fat, sweetened condensed milk
- ½ teaspoon vanilla extract

NUTRITIONAL ANALYSIS (PER TABLESPOON)

Calories 73 (11% from fat); Protein less than 1 gram; Carbohydrates 16 grams; Fiber less than 1 gram; Fat 1 gram.

Note: If a few sugar lumps do not dissolve, pour the warm sauce through a sieve and discard the lumps.

CHOCOLATE SAUCE

MAKES ¾ CUP

½ cup sugar

½ cup water

⅓ cup cocoa powder

⅓ cup sugar-free or low-calorie maple syrup

1 teaspoon vanilla extract

1 tablespoon light butter

Cocoa powder gives this sauce a very chocolatey taste. Light maple syrup gives a silky texture. It's hard to believe there is practically no butter in the sauce. Use this on low-fat ice cream or frozen yogurt or as a garnish for the fruit desserts in this chapter.

Combine sugar, water, and cocoa in a small saucepan and bring to a boil over medium-high heat. Stir frequently to avoid lumps. Reduce the heat and simmer for about 2 minutes.

Add maple syrup, vanilla, and butter and cook, stirring constantly, for about 2 minutes. Cool and store in a covered container.

**NUTRITIONAL ANALYSIS
(PER TABLESPOON)**

Calories 61 (15% from fat); Protein less than 1 gram;
Carbohydrates 13 grams; Fiber less than 1 gram; Fat 1 gram.

Index